I CHING: THE No. 1 SUCCESS FORMULA

Let this time-tested method help you make the right decisions today!

I Ching

The No. 1 Success Formula

Let this time-tested method help you
make the right decisions — today!

Christopher Markert

THE AQUARIAN PRESS

First published in the UK 1986

© CHRISTOPHER MARKERT 1986

British Library Cataloguing in Publication Data

Markert, Christopher
  I Ching: the no. 1 success formula.
  1. I Ching
  I. Title
  299'.51282   B127.12

  ISBN 0-85030-493-8

*The Aquarian Press is part of the Thorsons Publishing Group,
Wellingborough, Northamptonshire, NN8 2RQ England*

Printed in Great Britain by Richard Clay Limited, Bungay, Suffolk

10 9 8 7 6 5 4 3

CONTENTS

PART I

The I Ching

CHAPTER ONE

What this Book Can do for You

'How can I make a success of my next project?'; 'What can I do to make my present life more prosperous and fulfilling?'; 'How can I improve my relationship with the person I love?'; 'Which type of work will bring me the greatest financial and personal rewards?' Whenever you have questions like these, the I Ching can help you find meaningful answers.

Millions of people are using this amazing book as a practical guide in their daily lives. They consult it to decide important issues, to gain deeper insights and to widen their mental horizons. They refer to it when they need workable solutions in any area of life: at home, at work, in the family, in their social life and in their relationship with the opposite sex.

When you are confronted with puzzling alternatives, the I Ching can help you clear your mind and to arrive at the right decisions. Almost every time you open it you will find new and revealing ideas in it, although parts of the text are actually older than any other book in the world. This is truly a time-tested key to happiness and success, which has a profound and beneficial influence on practically everybody who studies it.

Instructions for looking up your answer follow in Chapter 3. Simplified instructions are found on page 276, at the very end of the book.

What do you expect from life, and what does the word success mean to you? This will be discussed in the next chapter. Other chapters will show why this ancient book is so effective in present-day practice and why even computer scientists and atomic physicists are now eager to learn from it.

But, you may ask, how can any book possibly do all these things? Chapter 6 will satisfy your curiosity and show you the inner workings of this ingenious system. Chapter 4 shows how the male–female relationship pervades your whole life, and how you can achieve harmony with the opposite sex. The entire book is, in fact, based on the polarity between male and female elements in all areas of life.

Until fifty years ago the I Ching was hardly known in the West, but in recent decades its popularity has been growing rapidly. Its usefulness and relevance has been acknowledged by experts in different fields. The world-famous Swiss psychologist Carl Gustav Jung studied it for years and found it a source of inexhaustible wisdom. Nobel-prize-winning physicist Niels Bohr recognized the parallels between the concepts of the I Ching and those of modern atomic science. He used the book's basic Yin–Yang symbol as a motif for his personal coat of arms. Physicist Fritjof Capra noted that change and transformation are the primary aspects of modern physics as well as those of the I Ching, as explained in his book *The Tao of Physics*. All these similarities have their deeper reasons, as you will see in Chapter 5. The principles of our modern calculus, on which computer science is based, were actually inspired by the I Ching some 300 years ago.

At present the I Ching is popularly known as a mysterious book that can be used as a party game or for fortune-telling. Few people are familiar with its deeper aspects. But its influence on our culture and way of life is destined to increase in the coming decades.

The text originated in China, and the title I Ching means 'The System of Changes'. During the past 5,000 years, millions of people all over the Orient have used the ideas contained in it to guide them in their pursuits and decisions. Men and women, kings and prophets, generals and farmers, poor people and rich have benefited from the practical wisdom that lies packed between its covers. By consulting it they became more aware of the ever-changing conditions around and within them. They learned to

'By consulting the I Ching they became more aware of the ever-changing conditions around and within them.'

move with life's current instead of against it, to see opportunities and avoid obstacles. The I Ching opened their eyes to the really important issues in their lives and advised them on the best course of action in the pursuit of their respective goals.

From its very inception many thousands of years ago, the I Ching was meant to serve as a practical guide for the more important issues of everyday life. But as time went on, it gained a reputation of being hard to understand, because the archaic language of the original text was no longer known to succeeding generations. Thus it became an obscure oracle, of interest mainly to mystics and students of the Far East.

The new edition you are reading now was written to bridge this time gap. It explains the ancient ideas and images in terms that modern readers can readily grasp and accept. It covers all facets of daily life, from the profound to the seemingly trivial. For instance, you may be plagued by a desire to eat food that is delicious but fattening. Do you deserve this tempting treat or should you resist? This may sound like a simple question, but it probably touches a deeper complex, and through the I Ching you will discover what it is.

The sixty-four answers (hexagrams) in Part II of the book are written in normal English that makes sense to the average modern reader. A figure of speech like 'stepping on the tiger's tail' would confuse most people today, although it was part of Chinese everyday language when the original text was written a long time ago. It simply means 'stirring up dangerous forces'. The ancient sages would have been just as confused by certain phrases we use today, such as 'reaching a bottleneck' or 'hitting a bull's-eye', for which they would have preferred the equivalent Chinese phrases.

At this point I should add a note about the illustrations. The original I Ching was, of course, written in the Chinese picture language. Some of the early editions rank as true works of art, composed by famous calligraphers. Because the Chinese express their thoughts in a sequence of pictographs, their literature is closely related to their art.

Most of the great Chinese artists were thoroughly familiar with the I Ching and the idea of change and balance in nature. Their works usually reflect cyclical changes in the weather, the seasons and the stages of growth. Each picture illustrates one aspect of 'Chi', the cosmic power and the subtle Yin–Yang balance in nature. According to a classic Chinese instruction manual for painters, the artist must first learn to still his/her heart, clarify his understanding and increase his wisdom. Thus, we can look upon each print in this book as on an illustration of inner and outer harmony that helps us to stay in touch with life.

Although the sixty-four answers (hexagrams) often use the masculine form (he, him, his) for reasons of convenience, the text should be understood in the widest sense, including both sexes. Especially the 'Changing Lines' in each hexagram can refer to the inquirer or to anyone else who comes to the inquirer's mind. A sentence like 'He needs intelligence as well' could thus refer to yourself, or to a partner, a friend or relative, or to some other person of either sex.

Note on Further Reading

This book will provide you with a comprehensive and practical guide to using the I Ching. For further study into the more profound aspects of the I Ching, the Wilhelm/Baynes translation is recommended.

Note on Quotations

All quotations in this edition are from the James Legge translation, published in England in 1899.

CHAPTER TWO

Success in the Widest Sense

To be truly successful as a human being it is not enough to make money and to improve your status. To be able to handle all levels and dimensions of your life, you have to find the right inner and outer balance. Many a so-called 'successful person' is really a human failure because he/she neglected certain essential areas.

Most important in our lives in undoubtedly our relationship with the opposite sex, whether we are aware of this or not. When our attitude in this respect is unrealistic, any success in other areas becomes incomplete and meaningless. The I Ching offers here a useful and time-tested concept that is unknown to most people in the West. The entire book is in fact based on the polarity between the male and the female principle, the *Yang* and the *Yin*. The text describes the changing relationship between the two cosmic forces that we perceive as day and night, heaven and earth, sun and moon, body and mind, reason and intuition, conscious and unconscious mind, male and female. Both forces are considered equally important, they complement and enhance each other. Both poles are 'good' when they harmonize with each other, and both of them show their vicious sides as soon as the harmony is lost. Our purpose of life is therefore not to suppress or defeat one or the other element, but to bring out the best in both of them. In this respect Chinese thinking differs radically from our fixed Western concepts that emphasize confrontation and superiority of one element over the other.

In practical terms this means that the I Ching has the ability to reconcile seemingly conflicting views and qualities. Many people in the West, for example, feel that the 'battle of the sexes' is

羅浮春夢

丙寅冬月
環中子畫

'Men and women were made to love and complement each other.'

natural and inevitable. Through the I Ching they suddenly realize that this conflict is only in their minds, and that men and women were made to love and complement each other. They also discover that there is no inherent conflict between mind and body – and that only a prejudiced mind would see a 'vessel of sin' in the body. By the same token the I Ching points out that our main purpose in life is not to go to heaven, but to create a 'heaven on earth' by harmonizing the Yin and Yang elements within us and around us.

This Chinese attitude, which is also shared by the Japanese to some extent, differs substantially from the one found in the Indo-European cultures, including our own. Even India and the Near East are 'Western' in this respect, they can be recognized by their idealistic and heaven-oriented teachings. In the Far East, on the other hand, we find a more practical and down-to-earth attitude, and this is why the I Ching opens new horizons for us.

The original text of the I Ching often refers to the 'noble sage' or the 'superior man' who sets an example of how the inquirer ought to think and act. The book's Great Commentary describes how such an enlightened person feels akin to the forces of heaven and earth, and how he/she therefore acts in harmony with them. He intuitively understands all creatures under the sun, and his attitude towards them is benevolent and helpful. He acts in tune with prevailing circumstances but is not carried away by them. Because he lives in harmony with the cosmic laws, he is centered within himself and has no secret doubts or worries. 'He rests in his own present position and cherishes the spirit of generous benevolence; and hence he can love without reserve.'

The enlightened person cultivates a balanced state of mind. He is in touch with the heaven above and the earth below and he forms a link between the two. He is equally at home in the spiritual sphere and the world of everyday activity. By being in tune with the cosmic forces he naturally does the right things and attains the right goals, without straining and without using force: 'With the attainment of such ease and such freedom from laborious effort, the mastery is got of all principles under the sky.'

But although he knows how to do the things that matter most at any given time and to reach the right goals, he does not take credit for his success: 'He toils with success but does not boast of it; he achieves merit but takes no virtue to himself from it.' This is because he knows that he enjoys the support of nature and that without this support he would accomplish little or nothing.

Accordingly he does not consider himself superior to other people. He treats them with respect and does not interfere in their private affairs. But by consistently improving his own character he has a beneficial influence on all people with whom he comes into contact.

The enlightened person follows the 'Tao' (the right path), as a matter of principle, even in the small details of everyday life – in contrast to the person who is still confused as to the true nature of things: 'The small man is not ashamed of what is not benevolent, nor does he fear to do what is not righteous. ... Self-correction, however, in what is small could make him careful in what would be of greater consequence.'

Through periods of solitude and meditation, the enlightened person cultivates a balanced state of mind. By maintaining a subtle inner balance of Yin and Yang, he/she is able to deal more effectively with the outer world and with other people: 'The superior man composes himself before he tries to move others; makes his mind restful and easy before he speaks; settles the principles of his intercourse with others before he seeks anything from them.' In this way he avoids situations where people will not respond to him because they sense that he is nervous and confused. Such a lack of co-operation would tend to deteriorate into unpleasant confrontations: 'When there are none in accord with him, those who work to injure him will make their appearance.'

The enlightened person 'knows how to secure the faith of others without the use of words, by setting an example of virtuous conduct.' But when he (or she) does speak, he uses cautious and subtle language. He realizes that words can have a far-reaching effect. Once a wrong thought has been expressed, it cannot be recalled, and the harm has been done. By the same token it is true that a right word spoken at the right time can practically move mountains.

'Through periods of solitude and meditation, the enlightened person cultivates a subtle inner balance of Yin and Yang.'

By being in tune with the universal and cosmic laws, the enlightened person feels at home in the world and understands all living creatures. His wisdom applies everywhere and his successes are not limited by space or time: 'It is thus that his operation is spirit-like, unconditioned by place, while the changes which he produces are not restricted to any form.'

To clear his mind and to decide important issues, the enlightened person relies on the I Ching for guidance, according to the Great Commentary: 'He asks the I Ching, making his inquiry in words. It receives his order, and the answer comes as the echo's response. Be the subject remote or near, mysterious or deep, he forthwith knows of what kind will be the coming developments.'

The I Ching can throw light on confusing situations and clear the path for realistic action. Thus, this book serves as a 'success manual' in the widest sense and in all areas of your life.

Now that you have the I Ching at your disposal, you can start applying the ancient success formula yourself. The following chapter explains how to consult the book, how to look up the answer to the question that concerns you most at the moment.

CHAPTER THREE

How to Consult the Book

To explore what is complex, search out what is hidden, to look up what lies deep, and reach to what is distant, thereby determining the issues for good or ill of all events under the sky, there is nothing greater than the I Ching. It exhibits the past and teaches us to discriminate the issues of the future. It makes manifest what is still small and brings to light what is obscure.

You have a question or a problem and you want a quick solution. The answer you are looking for is already within you, it is hidden in your unconscious mind, and the I Ching can help you bring it to light. But the insight can come to you only after you relax and calm your restless intellect. The really important issues in your life can come to the surface only when your conscious mind stops chattering away. But how can you reach that collected state of mind?

The I Ching provides for a little ceremony that helps you to relax and find your centre before you look up your answer in the book. This involves throwing three coins a number of times or sorting fifty sticks in a certain way. The main purpose of this ceremony is to get you into a receptive state of mind and let you focus on the issue that concerns you deep down and that you want to clarify. At the same time the coins or sticks help you find out which of the answers in the book deals with your present situation.

At first you will use the coin method because it is easier. Best suited for this are the unique ancient Chinese brass coins with a square hole in the centre. But you may find these difficult to

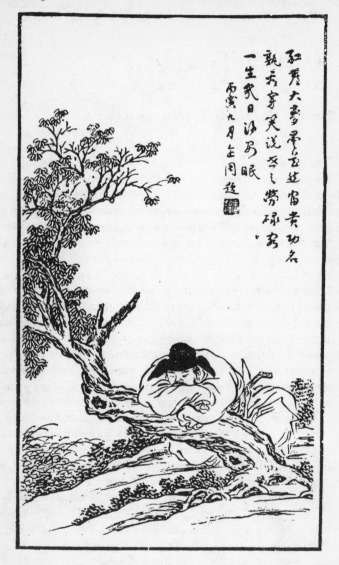

'The answer you are looking for is already within you, ... and the I Ching can help you recognize it.'

obtain; and in the meantime, three ordinary coins of the same size will do. More detailed instructions for the yarrow stalk method will follow in Chapter 8.

You start the ceremony by retiring to a quiet place where you will not be disturbed. Sit in a comfortable position, with the coins, writing material and the book in front of you. Formulate the question that concerns you most at the moment, such as: 'Should I trust Mr X in a certain matter?' or 'Is it advisable to move to such and such a place in two months?' or 'Shall I go ahead with a certain project now?'

Relax for a few minutes and ponder all aspects of your question with an open mind. Release all physical tension until you feel thoroughly at ease. Choose a posture that is comfortable but not slumping. Accept any relevent ideas or images that come to your mind, and avoid anxious or wishful thinking. Write your question down, in a few straightforward words. Your question can be specific (Shall I go ahead?), or more general and open to new insights (How shall I go about this?), or you can simply ask for guidance (The issue is...). Avoid double questions that would confuse the issue, such as: 'Would it be better to go on holiday now or should I start a new venture?' Include a time-span in your question where time is relevant. Example: 'Would it be wise to move to the city in two months?' Never use the I Ching for personal or financial gain at the expense of others. It is said that people who do this lose their ability to communicate with the book, and bring misfortune upon themselves.

Now you are ready to find your answer by throwing the coins and constructing your hexagram. Each hexagram is made up of six horizontal lines, some of them solid and others broken. There are sixty-four of these six-lined diagrams, and one of them applies to you at any given time.

An example:

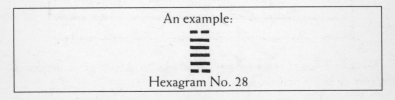

Hexagram No. 28

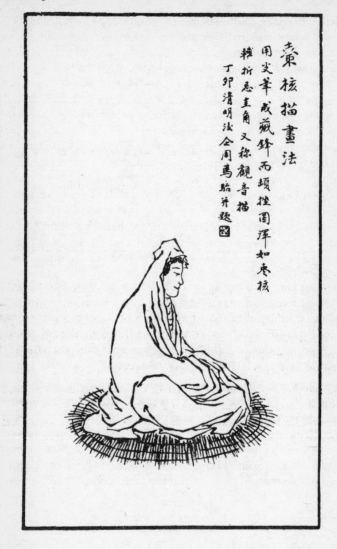

'Relax for a few minutes and ponder all aspects of your question with an open mind.'

Shake the three coins between your cupped hands for a few seconds and let them fall onto the table or a large flat surface. Four combinations of coins are possible, and each combination corresponds to a straight or divided line.*

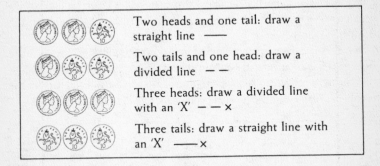

Two heads and one tail: draw a straight line ——

Two tails and one head: draw a divided line — —

Three heads: draw a divided line with an 'X' — — ×

Three tails: draw a straight line with an 'X' —— ×

Your first throw forms the bottom line of your hexagram. Throw the coins five more times and draw a line each time, one above the other. Remember that the column of six lines starts from the bottom, not from the top. As you keep throwing the coins and the hexagram gradually builds up, continue thinking about the question you would like to have answered.

Example: Suppose you have thrown the coins six times and have arrived at the following hexagram:
The fifth line (counting from the bottom up) is followed by an 'X', which will be explained on page 29.

* Other translations of the I Ching may use a more complicated method for determining the lines, involving the numbers 6, 7, 8 and 9, but the end result is the same.

By referring to the chart below you can now find the number of your hexagram, as follows. First, find the vertical column on the chart that contains the top three lines of your hexagram. In our example this would be ☷ x . These upper three lines are also called the 'Upper Trigram'. Next, find the horizontal bar in the chart that contains the bottom three lines of your hexagram, in our case ☷ . These three bottom lines are also called the 'Lower Trigram'.

Now trace the vertical column down to where it meets the horizontal bar and read the number at the crossing point. This is the number of your hexagram that you can now look up in the book. In our example you would look up Hexagram No. 22.

Upper Trigram →								
2	34	5	26	11	9	14	43
25	51	3	27	24	42	21	17
6	40	29	4	7	59	64	47
33	62	39	52	15	53	56	31
12	16	8	23	1	20	35	45
44	32	48	18	46	57	50	28
13	55	63	22	36	37	30	49
10	54	60	41	19	61	38	58

Chart for looking up your hexagram

When reading the text of your hexagram, take your time, relax and note the subtle clues that the I Ching has to offer. Look for the wider meaning of words and sentences as they relate to your question. Some of the sentences may puzzle you at first, but will reveal their meaning minutes later. Sometimes the flash of insight will come hours or even days later.

After you have consulted the I Ching on several occasions, you will discover that the text has many dimensions. In typical Chinese fashion, a question that you have asked on one level may be answered on another level. For instance, if you ask: 'Is he (or she) in love with me?', the I Ching may reply: 'There has not yet been any harm from a selfish wish to influence.' You may interpret this to mean that the important thing in your love relationship is not whether you are being loved, but whether the love is pure and unselfish on both sides.

In this way, the text can help you to transcend your narrow frame of reference and open up another dimension in which your question answers itself. Readers who are not familiar with the Far-Eastern mentality and who are used to the straight, one-dimensional Western way of thinking may find this confusing at first. But most of our frustrations in life are, in fact, created by our lack of flexibility and mental agility. This is why many problems that seem insurmountable to a set mind tend to dissolve into thin air when viewed from a more realistic angle.

Another example will illustrate this. Suppose you want to start a business project and you ask: 'How can I finance this venture?' The I Ching answers: 'We must look at those whom we are seeking to nourish.' Your attention is now shifted to the final purpose of your venture, which is presumably to 'feed' someone, or to support yourself and/or others. The financing of your venture now suddenly appears secondary, and you remember why you want to start the venture in the first place. With this insight you may be able to find better and more efficient ways of 'nourishing' or supporting, – or the question of finance may resolve itself more easily when it is related to the final purpose.

As soon as you follow the clues and become aware of the real issue, an unexpected answer often presents itself on a higher level of understanding. Sometimes you may get the impression that the book has a sense of humour and is teasing you. At other times you may feel that you have received a rebuke. But as long as you approach the I Ching only on important occasions and with significant questions, you will receive a meaningful answer.

'When the question involves a joint project or is of general interest, you can consult the I Ching together with the people involved.'

Please note: If you get an answer that does not seem to apply to your situation, the chances are that you have not attuned yourself to the issue at hand, that you are not relaxed or have not considered all the ramifications of your question.

The Changing Lines

The last part of your hexagram text is entitled 'Changing Lines', and refers to the lines marked with an 'X'. In our example the fifth line (counting from the bottom) is changing, and you would refer to the corresponding text entitled 'Fifth Line'. This text gives you an idea of impending developments in your life. In other words: the first part of your hexagram describes your life as it is now, while the last part indicates what might develop next.

If your hexagram contains one or more changing lines (marked with an 'X'), draw now a new hexagram in which the line(s) reverts to its opposite. In our example the transformation would look like this:

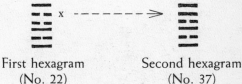

First hexagram
(No. 22)

Second hexagram
(No. 37)

By looking up this second hexagram as well, you receive additional clues on trends and possibilities coming up in the near or far future. You are now made aware of opportunities or dangers awaiting you, and you find advice on how to deal with unexpected developments. These are not firm predictions, of course. They merely indicate possibilities to watch out for. Armed with this information you are in a better position to shape your future.

In the second hexagram (No. 37 in our example) you would skip the hexagram text entitled 'Changing Lines'.

You may find the text referring to 'Changing Lines' ambiguous at first. Most of it is written in the 'he' form, although it should be understood in the widest sense, including both sexes. The context will help you decide to whom a particular changing line refers: to yourself, a partner, a friend or relative, or to some other person.

This concludes the chapter on how to consult the I Ching. In the future you can look up your hexagram by using the 'Instructions for Quick Reference' on page 276).

Now that you know how to use the I Ching in practice, let us discuss the basic idea on which this book rests, namely the Yin–Yang polarity.

CHAPTER FOUR

Male–Female, Yin–Yang

May we not say that Yang and Yin, or the undivided and divided lines, are the secret and substance of the I Ching.

This entire book rests on the Yin–Yang concept, on the polarity between male and female elements in all areas of life. The very fact that our Western languages have no equivalent for this concept is significant. It demonstrates the 'blind spot' in our culture when it comes to the balance between man and woman, logic and intuition, thoughts and feelings, mind and body, activity and rest, father and mother, heaven and earth, etc. Very few Western thinkers seem to have noticed this gap until recently, but a growing number has become aware of it within the last decades. Ralph Waldo Emerson was one of the first to deal with the subject. In his essays he spoke of the polarity that we can see everywhere in nature: in darkness and light, north and south, male and female, in the rhythm of the blood and the vibrations of sounds.

Everything in Nature is divided, so that everything is a half that must be completed by another thing: spirit and matter, man and woman, subjective and objective, inside and outside, above and below, yes and no. ... The whole system of things is represented in every part. In each creature there is something that reminds us of the ebb and flow of the oceans, of day and night, of man and woman.

Emerson shared the Far-Eastern belief that the two poles complement each other, that they are both equally important, and that a dynamic balance exists between them. Most Western philosophies and scriptures, on the other hand, tend to glorify one pole and neglect the other. For instance, they consider the mind to be better than the body, logic better than intuition, heaven better than earth, and the 'Heavenly Father' better than the 'Mother Earth'. Accordingly, our culture emphasizes male values and degrades many of the female values. Here lies the main reason why so many Western women reject the female role: they sense that female qualities are considered inferior in our Yang-oriented culture. But because they are themselves part of this society, they practise in effect a form of hidden male chauvinism, and they try to acquire male qualities. Although the Chinese culture is not free of sexism, it is more Yin-oriented as a whole.

The Far-Eastern Yin–Yang concept can help us to gain a healthier balance between the sexes and a saner attitude towards Nature, towards the body and the unconscious mind. Our attitude towards the unconscious is crucial to our mental balance. Any long-term friction or repression in this area produces symptoms of neurosis. A certain friction is, in fact, built into our Western culture. All of us suffer from this 'cultural neurosis' to a greater or lesser extent. The Freudian teachings have added to the problem by telling us that the unconscious mind is a 'cesspool of chaotic emotions'. In the Far-Eastern view, the unconscious values are to a great extent represented by the 'inner self' that acts as a powerful ally and becomes destructive only when the conscious mind loses its balance.

But the Western cultures have not always been lop-sided. Our present male-oriented scale of values is a comparatively recent phenomenon, in historical terms. Many prehistoric societies in Europe and the Near East were more balanced, as scientists are now finding out. But few written records remain from these periods. In the Far East, however, we are fortunate to find in the I Ching a 5,000-year-old text that preserves the ancient values.

Such a natural male–female balance is also described in Japanese mythology, which was influenced by Chinese concepts. According to Japanese legend, the world was created by 'Izanagi' and 'Izanani', the primeval father and mother. Their love relationship and sexual union is innocently described in every detail. This legend is the basis of a joyful and spontaneous nature worship that can be observed in Japan to this day. In the Japanese mind, the earth and the sea, the mountains and the forests, and nature herself, are born of the sacred union between the male and the female spirit. Accordingly, the most important religious structure in Japan is the Ise Shrine, dedicated to the sun goddess Ise, and the Japanese emperor is considered her descendant. This innocent faith in nature explains in part the incredible vitality and resilience of the Japanese people, although in recent centuries a more patriarchal and militaristic philosophy has been superimposed on the ancient beliefs.

A similar shift toward patriarchy and male values has also occurred in China in the course of centuries. Even in ancient texts like the I Ching we have to distinguish between the original and later additions, commentaries and translations. Some of the Confucian commentaries, for example, are slightly male-oriented. A shift away from the original text in very early times is also noticeable in the sequence of the first two hexagrams, and in their titles. In the translations available today, the first hexagram describes the Yang (male) force and is usually entitled 'The Creative'. Hexagram No. 2 describes the Yin (female) force and is most often called 'The Receptive'. Both the titles and the sequence might be interpreted to imply an obvious value judgement in favour of the male.

An earlier version of the I Ching from the Shang Dynasty (1766–1122 BC) lists the Yin (female) hexagram first and uses no titles. My own feeling is that this version is not only more authentic, but also more logical, because in Chinese cosmology the Yin is traditionally listed before the Yang. For instance, the all-encompassing 'Chi' (the cosmos or absolute) is always given the number 1. Next comes the Earth or the Yin principle with the number 2, and Heaven or the Yang principle carries the number 3. All even numbers in Chinese numerology are therefore considered Yin, all odd numbers Yang. Just as, in building a house, the foundation is laid before the roof is constructed, it makes sense that, in creating the cosmos, the earth should materialize before heaven. The same down-to-earth mentality caused the authors of the I Ching to construct each hexagram from the bottom up, not from the top down.

From all this it seems obvious that the original text of the I Ching was altered some centuries before Confucius, with the intention of degrading the Yin (female) element and upgrading the Yang (male) element. In the present edition I have restored the original sequence. I have also taken the liberty of rephrasing other male-oriented statements wherever I found them throughout the book. I did not do this so much in an attempt to be fair to the female sex, but because I feel that such statements are against the inner logic of the I Ching, against human nature and against my own nature. The sex bias in our own or any other culture hurts men just as much as it does women.

The basic meaning of the Yin/Yang polarity is usually described as 'shady/sunny', 'gentle/firm', or 'female/male'. Yang is often pictured as a winged dragon which roams the heavens and initiates things. Yin is represented as a mare: graceful, patient, fertile, capable of giving and maintaining life.

Yang is strong, vigorous, undeflected, correct, and in all these qualities pure, unmixed, exquisite. Yin is gentle and flexible but, when put in motion is determined and persistent. It is still, but able to give every definite form. It contains all things in itself, and its transforming power is glorious. It receives the influences of heaven and acts at the proper time.

When Yin shows its undesirable aspects, it becomes shapeless, passive, chaotic, shady, negative, nagging and small-minded. It can lose the wider perspective and waste its time on petty details and routines.

When Yang shows its undesirable aspects, it becomes rigid, arrogant, aggressive, brutal, fanatical, narrow-minded, impatient, top-heavy, lonely and sterile. It can lose touch with reality and the earth, and can waste energy on fanatical schemes and lofty ideals.

These undesirable qualities usually emerge in Yin and Yang simultaneously when the balance between them is disturbed. For instance, Yin will tend to become chaotic and negative as soon as

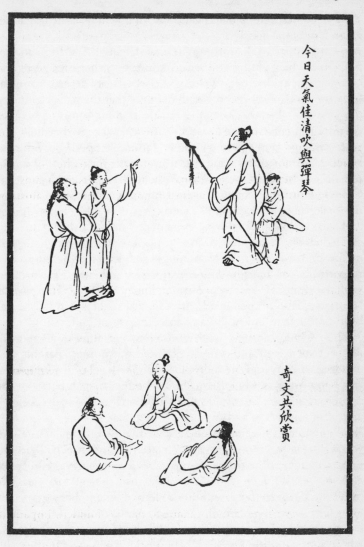

'The I Ching can help us to find a new harmony ... between men and women, fathers and mothers, parents and children.'

Yang becomes rigid and arrogant. Or Yang will become impatient when Yin is too passive.

From this broad definition of Yin and Yang it can be seen that both have their strong and weak points, and that they need and complement each other. When some translators describe Yang as 'creative' and Yin as 'receptive' they imply that the male element is the source of life that uses the female as a mere tool. This idea corresponds, of course, to our Western image of the male god who creates the world without female help. The Chinese language, on the other hand, has no word for 'God'. It only speaks of Chi, the Absolute, which manifests itself as Yin and Yang. The Chinese word that comes closest to our concept of 'God' is Yang, the male half of creation. Westerners are in effect worshipping half of creation and ignoring or suppressing the other half. This one-sided, single-minded approach has brought us much success in the areas of science, technology and warfare. But it is also responsible for most of our frustrations and neuroses, for our artificial way of life and our declining vitality. The typical Westerner is so preoccupied with external success that he/she has little time left to enjoy life and to take care of children.

The I Ching can help us to find a new harmony in all areas of life, between man and woman, father and mother, parents and children, society and the individual. On the level of the individual this knowledge can help us to find a better balance between the conscious and the unconscious mind, thoughts and feelings, logic and intuition, body and mind.

Women can thus make good use of their Yang (male) qualities while normally relying on the Yin (female) approach. Without becoming masculine they can apply Yang traits such as enterprise and logic. And men can make good use of Yin qualities like intuition and sensitivity without becoming effeminate.

As long as we maintain our Yang-oriented attitude, we will tend to suppress our feelings, degrade the body and use rigid logic where subtle intuition is called for. We will feel lonely in the cold, rational world that we have created for ourselves. The relationship between the sexes will remain artificial and superficial, the balance between father and mother will be disturbed, and children will no longer fit into our world. We will continue to suffer from inner conflicts, hate, guilt and regret, and we will project these feelings onto our relatives, acquaintances, friends, neighbours and the whole world. This tense atmosphere will give rise to social and military conflicts. But by becoming aware of the distortion in our picture of the world we can find the way to a happier future.

The next chapter will explain how even modern scientists find fault with the Western picture of reality, whereas they discover in the I Ching many truths that agree with their latest scientific theories.

CHAPTER FIVE

Modern Science and the I Ching

... the sages searched out exhaustively what was deep, and investigated the minutest springs of things.

Psychologists like C.G. Jung discovered profound truths in the I Ching. Even atomic physicists, among them Nobel-prize-winners, have recently found that this seemingly unscientific book can teach them something. For instance, the idea that 'everything changes' agrees with their concept of the world on the atomic and subatomic level. Electrons, atoms, particles and waves are forever moving and transforming, in a continuously changing interrelationship – just like the lines, trigrams and hexagrams in the I Ching. While the traditional Western models of reality are preoccupied with absolute values and stable relationships, the world of physics, and that of the I Ching, never stands still.

Furthermore, physicists are aware of the dual aspect of matter on the atomic level. Matter can manifest as waves or as particles, depending on the situation. In the I Ching, the cosmic energy also appears in two different forms that can transform into each other, namely Yin and Yang. A solid (Yang) line in a hexagram can change into a broken (Yin) line, and vice versa.

Another aspect of the I Ching that appeals to modern physicists is the relation between spirit and matter. The Chinese believe that spirit and matter are two aspects of the same thing. To them, spirit is inherent in matter. They do not see matter as a passive object that must be moved by an external spiritual force or by God, as in the traditional Western model of reality. Einstein's field theory agrees with the I Ching. It states that the natural laws are not externally imposed on things, but are immanent in them. In the same way the lines in a hexagram, and the events symbolized by them, change by themselves, out of inner logic.

A further parallel between Far-Eastern teachings and modern physics is the belief that all our words, concepts and models of reality are only makeshift tools with limited applicability. A particular concept may be perfectly logical and 'scientific' in itself, but it is still a mere model of reality. Even our languages, our sciences and our mathematics can only circumscribe reality – they can never grasp reality itself. Orientals, and students of Zen in particular, have always been aware of this, and Lao Tzu said in his famous Tao Te Ching 2,500 years ago: 'The truth that can be put into words is not the eternal truth. Only relative things can be expressed in words, and all descriptions are only comparisons.' The I Ching is ideally suited to demonstrate the relativity of our conceptual knowledge and to free us from our narrow frames of reference. It also shows us that our intuition can often lead us to scientific discoveries, as physicists like Einstein, Niels Bohr and Heisenberg have often pointed out.

Thus we find that the traditional Western models of reality disagree with the scientific facts in many respects. At the same time several of our top scientists realize that the ancient I Ching comes surprisingly close to the truth. Even the very key to all life on earth bears an amazing resemblance to the structure of the I Ching: the sixty-four hexagrams correspond exactly to the sixty-four DNA codons of the genetic code, as described in *The Hidden Key to Life* by Martin Schonberger.

In the field of medicine we are also beginning to learn from the Chinese concepts that were originally inspired by the I Ching. Oriental healers emphasize prevention and maintaining the Yin–Yang balance in the body. The better Chinese doctors used to get paid a fixed monthly rate for keeping the client healthy. Whenever the client got ill, the payment was withheld and the doctor paid for all treatments and medicines until health was restored. It was the job of the doctor to detect irregularities in the very beginning stages and to be aware of the root causes of disease:

'Oriental healers emphasize prevention and maintaining the Yin–Yang balance in the body.'

He traces things to their beginning and follows them to their end; thus he knows what can be said about death and life. He perceives how the union of essence and breath form things, and how the disappearance or wandering away of the soul produces the change of their constitution. (From the I Ching)

Western medicine, on the other hand, is disease-oriented and mainly concerned with the suppression of symptoms through chemicals and surgery. Modern medical books list hundreds of thousands of diseases, with all their symptoms and complications, but they say little or nothing about health and how to maintain it. By the same token modern patients have been conditioned to expect doctors to perform quick (and expensive) repair jobs. Very few people today would be ready to admit that most illnesses can be prevented through a healthier way of life, and that they themselves are therefore to blame for most of their illnesses.

In the West, and particularly in the USA, medicine is big business, and the profitable medical-pharmaceutical complex keeps growing, while the quality of public health keeps declining year by year. Medical and hospital expenses are rising to astronomical levels, while the list of degenerative diseases gets longer and longer. Vital parts of the body like the heart, the liver, the blood vessels, the intestines or the joints deteriorate without visible cause. One out of every four Americans will contract cancer in the course of his/her life.

Doctors find themselves helpless in the face of this growing avalanche of diseases, and many of them get ill from stress, frustration and overwork. But this is not all. Authors like Ivan Illich have noted that many of today's diseases are actually caused by the doctors and their methods. To the long list of miseries from which modern mankind suffers, we now have to add the 'iatrogenic diseases' (iatros = doctor, genic = caused). Huge sums are spent to repair the damages brought about by modern drugs and surgery. To stay in hospital does not only get more expensive every year, but also more dangerous. Nowhere is the risk of infection by virulent bacteria as high as in our modern hospitals. People who are brought there in a weakened condition must count on all kinds of complications.

Slowly we are coming to the conclusion that we cannot expect too much from modern medicine, even though it often performs miracles, and even though we would not want to get along without it. We remember Hippocrates, the founder of modern medicine, who said two thousand years ago: 'The doctor can treat a disease, but only Nature can heal.' In our desperate situation we begin to experiment with alternative methods of natural healing, with preventative and holistic medicine. Strange Far-Eastern methods are being investigated by teams of Western doctors. People begin to rediscover their bodies and to pay more attention to nutrition, about which most Western doctors have learned little or nothing in medical school. People try to live and eat more naturally, and to avoid overly refined foods. There is a growing interest in Far-Eastern therapies like acupressure, shiatzu, do-in and foot-reflexology that help to support the body's inherent self-healing powers.

The I Ching teaches us that, when it comes to our health, we must watch our daily habits and listen to the signals from the body. Most of our serious illnesses evolve slowly in the course of many years, and are the result of countless small neglects, as it says in the I Ching:

> *The small man thinks that small acts of goodness are of no benefit, and does not do them; and that small deeds of evil do no harm, and does not abstain from them. Hence his wickedness becomes great till it cannot be covered, and his guilt becomes greater till it cannot be pardoned.*

People who believe in prevention in any area of life are aware of the future. They know that the world around them and within them is forever moving, changing and transforming, and they know how to influence future developments in the beginning stage. Very few Western thinkers have touched upon this subject, but the Greek philosopher Heraclitus used the phrase 'Panta Rei' (everything moves) to express the gist of his teachings. More recently, atomic physicists came to the same conclusion, as we have seen. Generally speaking, however, Western people live in a

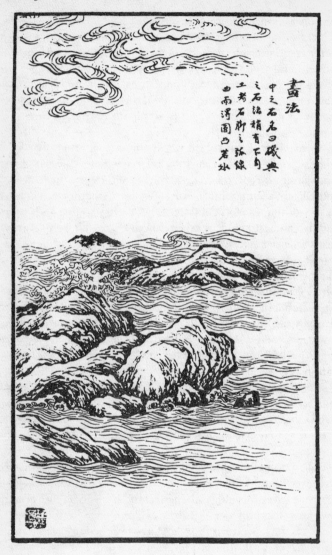

'Change is inherent in the cosmic order, and we should be prepared for it and move with the currents of life.'

static mental world where 'everything has its place'.

The Chinese, on the other hand, have always felt that change is inherent in the cosmic order, and that we should be prepared for it and move with the currents of life. Accordingly, they called their oldest and most influential scripture 'The System of Changes' – which is the book you are reading now, and which states:

> *Does not he who knows the spring of things possess spirit-like wisdom? ...*
> *Those springs are the slight beginnings of movement, and the earliest*
> *indications of good fortune or ill. The superior man sees them, and acts*
> *accordingly without waiting a single day. ... Yea, moreover, if we wish*
> *to know what is likely to be preserved and what to perish, what will be*
> *lucky and what will be unlucky, this may easily be known from the*
> *explanations of the different lines of the hexagram.*

In the Chinese cosmology all things complement each other in a continuously shifting Yin–Yang balance. An obvious example of this is the movement of the sun, moon and stars. We experience corresponding changes in the weather, the seasons, the tides, the plants and animals, in ourselves and in the people around us. Our own emotions may change from one minute to the next, and our relationships with others are equally subject to change.

Thus, the Chinese 'Science of Change', together with our own modern science, can help us to become more aware of these cosmic forces and their tendencies within us and around us. By anticipating impending changes we can stay in tune with life, and our actions can become more appropriate and effective. In the next chapter we will analyse the I Ching further and find out why it is so useful in everyday life.

CHAPTER SIX

How the Method Works

Anciently, when the sages made the I Ching, it was with the design that its figures should be in conformity with the principles underlying the natures of men and things, and the ordinances appointed for them by heaven.

In the Far East, the I Ching is generally accepted as a source of profound wisdom. But any Westerner who encounters it for the first time is bound to find it somewhat confusing and strange. Even those who try it out and get meaningful results will tend to have their doubts about it.

Does it really work? And if so, why does it work? As an intelligent reader you have a right to know why it does. In this chapter we will take a sober look at the I Ching to find out what makes it so effective. This has never really been done before, and the very idea may shock some people. When I talked about my plan to analyse the book, to a friend of mine who teaches Chinese literature in Taiwan, she exclaimed: 'Oh, but that is impossible! Nobody will ever know how it works. It is just too deep and ancient.'

I can readily understand her feelings, and I agree that there are things in life which the intellect alone cannot explain and which we can only grasp intuitively. The Chinese have cultivated this sixth sense much more than we in the West. On the other hand it is no secret that they often rely too much on intuition, at the expense of logic. In recent history they have begun to make up for this by adopting a more scientific approach. Technology, mass production and communism are some of the mixed blessings they have taken over from the West.

But there is no real contradiction between logic and intuition. We need both to be fully human. Cultures or individuals who depend too much on one or the other get into trouble sooner or later. Most of our own troubles, for example, can be traced to our overemphasis on the rational approach to life. For centuries we have been taught to ignore our feelings, to 'use our heads' and to despise our bodies. We have lost touch with ourselves, our roots and our intuitive talents.

This is one reason why we can benefit from books like the I Ching, which liberate us from our top-heavy habits and narrow frames of reference. We need not, however, accept such oriental teachings blindly and throw our intellect overboard.

On the contrary, we can often use our Western intellect to clarify Eastern ideas and to weed out superstitions and emotional overgrowth. In this way both East and West can benefit. In the case of the I Ching I found that I was even more impressed by it after I had taken it apart and analysed it with a critical eye. While doing this, I often felt like the boy who was given a watch for Christmas and took it apart the same evening to see what made it tick. Similarly, I had my doubts as to whether the I Ching would still work after I put it together again. I must admit that I conducted some disrespectful experiments with it that would have shocked many a Chinese sage. But I think the original authors would have approved, or they would not have called the book 'The System of Changes'. A system is, after all, supposed to be logical and accessible to the human intellect. In any case, the I Ching lived through my tests and came out more solid and brilliant than ever. The results I now get from it seem even more relevant because I no longer have secret doubts about it. While all earlier explanations by other authors left me dissatisfied, I am now fully convinced that the I Ching is based on a solid system that really works.

Previous Explanations

Here is how authors and commentators of past editions have tried to explain the inner workings of the I Ching:

James Legge, the Oxford scholar who translated the text in 1882, sometimes doubted that the book could work at all, although he admired its structure and accumulated wisdom. He suspected that the first authors had used divination as a pretext for teaching their philosophy.

Richard Wilhelm, the German sinologist, made the book his life's work. His comprehensive translation was first published in 1923. It does a remarkable job of clarifying the original text, although the arrangement is somewhat confusing. But beyond this, it gives no explanation of how the book works in practice. Presumably Wilhelm believed, as do most Chinese, that the I Ching is beyond human comprehension.

But **Carl G. Jung**, the famous Swiss psychologist who wrote the introduction to the Richard Wilhelm edition, did give an explanation. He describes how he studied the book intensively for many years, and how he often spent hours sitting under an old tree and getting his questions answered by looking up hexagrams. The answers never failed to bring surprising and enlightening mental associations; they threw light on confusing issues and helped him to see the deeper aspects of things. He explained this through a phenomemon that he called the 'law of synchronicity'. He believed that this law causes certain events to happen simultaneously in the world of matter and in the world of the spirit. Thus, when he arrived at a certain hexagram at a certain moment in time, this event corresponded in his opinion to simultaneous events in other areas of life, which made the hexagram relevant. As we shall see, this argument is not valid, although it contains a grain of truth.

R.L. Wing, in her translation of the I Ching, goes along with C.G. Jung. She also believes that the event of throwing the coins coincides with simultaneous events around the reader, through the 'law of synchronicity'.

Stan Gooch, the English psychologist, mentions the I Ching in

'The I Ching is based on a solid system that really works.'

most of his books, and he comes to this conclusion:

> *Through the I Ching we apparently gain access to the dimensions of eternity in which the limits of time and space are transcended. I personally have not the slightest idea of how such a book could be put together from scratch, and neither does anyone else. But the fact is that this mysterious book brings practical results.*

John Blofeld's condensed translation was first published in 1963. The author believes that the book is the manifestation of an unknown and unknowable omnipotent reality. He also states that perhaps the reader's subconscious (which may have access to the collective unconscious) contributes to the answers, and that divine inspiration plays its part.

Conclusions

When I started experimenting with the I Ching, I asked myself questions like: 'Can the I Ching really predict the future?' I concluded that the book is not so much an oracle that predicts the future, but a catalyst that makes us aware of present, past and future trends. It helps us to revive our instinct for recognizing the first beginning stages of developments and their likely outcome. Although our intellect can perceive certain aspects of the future, we need our all-encompassing intuitive faculties to grasp the wider context of things. While the intellect tends to perceive events in logical sequence, our intuition sees them in broad images that often include the beginning and the end, or the here and there. This is perhaps what Carl G. Jung had in mind when he spoke of synchronicity. But I believe that it is not so much the I Ching that transcends time and space, but our own intuition when inspired by the text. Another factor that can bring about seemingly simultaneous events within us and around us is our own conscious and unconscious desire, which focuses our attention on things and events that seem interconnected in time and space. Example: As soon as I get interested in a certain type of product, I see this product advertised and displayed in places where I never saw it before. This is a common occurrence which need not be explained through a law of synchronicity or divine providence.

My next question was: 'Is the I Ching really a manifestation of divine truth?' I found that the I Ching does not reveal the truth in objective terms, but that it triggers subjective mental associations which are relevant to our particular situation at a particular time. It follows from this that only you can interpret your hexagram. Nobody else can do it for you – and neither can you interpret for anyone else. An example may illustrate this: Suppose you throw the coins and arrive at a hexagram that says 'Inside the rough stone is a core of beautiful jade. The wise man polishes the jade.' You could conclude from this that your present project has great potential and that it will become beautiful if you refine it. Someone else may interpret the same text to mean that his or her own qualities are hidden and should be cultivated. A third person may say that the text refers to a certain introverted acquaintance of his. A fourth person may think that it means we should not rely on outer appearances. If you yourself had arrived at the same hexagram under different circumstances or in a different frame of mind, you would probably have come up with yet another answer. In each case the I Ching may be said to have revealed the 'divine truth' that was already dormant in the reader.

Next, I wanted to find an answer to the question: 'Can the coins or stalks really determine the one and only hexagram that applies at the moment?' It is unlikely that coins or stalks of any kind are endowed with magic powers that select the 'right' hexagram for us at a given time. Neither did I find any evidence of a mysterious law of synchronicity at work, which connects the event of coin-throwing with other simultaneous events around us or within us.

Instead, it is our own conscious and unconscious minds that interact with the text to produce relevant answers. The ceremony of handling the coins and stalks helps us to get into a receptive and collected state of mind. The minutes we spend in sorting and counting these paraphernalia allow us to calm down, to focus on the question we have asked and to become more aware of the issues involved. Sudden flashes of intuition let us see how the pieces of our puzzle fit together. Seemingly unconnected

'Is the I Ching a manifestation of divine truth?'

simultaneous events suddenly appear relevant. Other events that looked like mere coincidences a minute ago suddenly reveal their inner logic. Any hexagram can actually produce this effect, as long as the reader takes it seriously.

I took the liberty of proving this by purposely looking up the wrong hexagrams for friends, and telling them about it later. Invariably, the answers obtained from the 'wrong' text were just as relevant as those received from the 'right' hexagram. In other words, the important factor is not which hexagram we look up, but whether we are in the proper frame of mind when we read any hexagram.

The rules of the game in the I Ching have been ingeniously devised to make us focus on the relevant issues and to bring out our intuitive abilities. Through the ceremonious process of consulting the book we cultivate a certain state of mind or attitude, without which the method could not work in practice. By helping us to harmonize with our inner self, the book enables us to stay in tune with life and with the nature of things. The ancient authors of the I Ching realized that most human problems are not primarily caused by external obstacles, but by the way in which we react to these obstacles. This is why the text reminds us frequently to 'order our hearts', to 'compose ourselves', and to 'live in accordance with the cosmic order'. We are to follow the 'Tao', the right path in harmony with nature, and to observe the balance of Yin and Yang within us and around us. Modern psychologists would say that the book helps us to co-ordinate our conscious mind with the unconscious, our thoughts with our feelings, our logic with our intuition.

Recent research has thrown additional light on the way in which the human mind functions. It was found that each of the two sides of the brain has a different function. The left hemisphere functions more in a logical, analytical, verbal and mathematical way; it is more outer-oriented, 'masculine' and 'Western' and represents our Yang-nature. The right hemisphere functions more on the intuitive, imaginative, artistic and all-encompassing level; it is more inner-oriented, 'feminine' and 'oriental' and represents our Yin-nature. Because the nerve trains

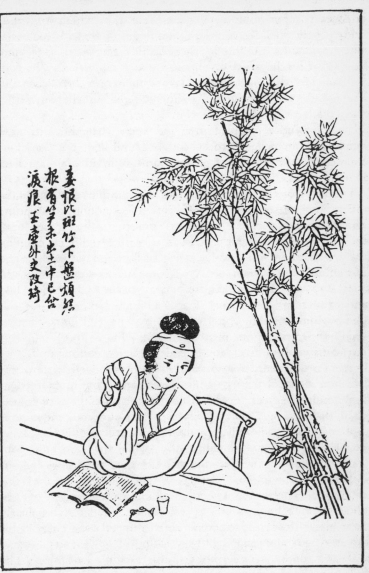

'The I Ching makes us focus on the relevant issues and brings out our intuitive abilities.'

cross each other upon leaving the brain, the right half of your body is controlled by your left brain hemisphere, and vice versa. The implications of this in everyday life are worth explaining here, because they have given rise to much confusion. Why is it, for example, that most people favour their right hand over the left? And why does the political right usually favour a conservative approach?

The answer is simple when we know that the left brain hemisphere (which controls the right hand) does our conscious thinking in everyday life. In other words, our (left brain) intellect is more at ease in an orderly, logical world that can easily be manipulated by the right hand. Our more intuitive (right) brain, on the other hand, favours the heart, the emotions and natural arrangements, which do not always conform to the rigid order of the intellect. Thus we are often faced with a right–left conflict, and we have to find a creative synthesis between our intellect and our intuition, between our conscious and unconscious needs. This, of course, is also the main purpose of the I Ching. The 'odd and mysterious' archetypal images in each hexagram give our unconscious mind an opportunity to express itself in a coherent way and to restore our mental balance. This, in turn, helps our intellect to regain its creativity and its contact with reality.

Successful leaders, creators and inventors are well aware of the fact that many of their best ideas are sparked by intuitive (right brain) hunches. Such ideas come out of the blue; they are not the result of logical reasoning. They usually occur while the mind is at ease but subconsciously focused on an urgent question. Some people get their most creative ideas while they are busy with some insignificant or rhythmic task like shaving, dishwashing or walking. (Throwing and sorting coins would fall into the same category.) There are several well-known examples of this phenomenon. Thomas Edison, the famous inventor, frequently came up with new ideas while 'dozing' in an easy chair in his office. Albert Einstein liked to spend up to twelve hours a day in bed, and ponder over scientific problems while half asleep. The inventor of the sewing machine and the discoverer of the benzine molecule structure both found their solutions while waking up and remembering dreams. Most of us have had comparable experiences that throw light on the way in which the subconscious mind comes up with relevant answers. The ceremony of consulting the I Ching creates the conditions that mobilize our intuitive powers.

The I Ching also helps us to absorbe advice easily and gradually. Instead of overwhelming us with a mass of material all at once, it feeds us one hexagram at a time, whenever we need guidance and inspiration most. In a way, this book can be seen as a collection of sixty-four essays covering all aspects of life and all stages of the cycles of life. Each hexagram looks at life from a different angle while covering all aspects of life, and it can therefore be related to any given human situation. For example, we are always interested in getting ahead (Hexagram 34), and we also want to slow down periodically (Hexagram 5). We have to deal with violent changes now and then (Hexagram 51), and we want to retain a pure heart (Hexagram 25), and so on.

But when we feel frustrated and need advice, to which hexagram should we turn? Literally, this is a 'toss up', because all of them apply. We could, of course, choose a hexagram at random. But through the coin ceremony we are relieved of this choice, and we get the feeling that fate has decided for us. This feeling may be entirely irrational, but it adds to the effect. We can now concentrate on the chosen hexagram with a single mind. Our inner uncertainty, which made us consult the I Ching in the first place, can now subside as we direct our attention to the search for the answer that seems to be hidden in the text, but that is really dormant in our own mind.

My next question was: 'Is the structure of the I Ching really beyond human understanding?' I came to the conclusion that the all-encompassing and multi-dimensional nature of the hexagrams is mainly due to the Yin–Yang concept, which lets us see the polarity in all areas of life. This concept is, in fact, a version of the binary system found in the human brain, and that is now also used in computers. The word 'binary' means twofold. In the case of the brain, the two basic units of input are Yes and No. In the case of the computer, the units are Zero and One, or Plus and Minus.

Curiously enough, the invention of modern calculus, which made the computer possible, was originally inspired by the I Ching. When the German mathematician Leibniz was shown a copy of the book over 200 years ago, he immediately recognized the advantage of the binary system over our traditional decimal system. Consequently he developed the corresponding tables that are now used in computer science.

Just as a giant computer can store an incredible amount of data in the form of electronic plus/minus impulses, so the hexagrams contain a wealth of wisdom, expressed by combinations of solid or broken lines. A solid (Yang) line means Plus, or Yes, or Above, or Firm, or Active, or Visible, or Heaven, or Male, depending on the context in the hexagram. A broken (Yin) line means Minus, or No, or Below, or Gentle, or Responsive, or Hidden, or Earth, or Female, again depending on the context.

This grid of polarities can span the entire spectrum between the two extremes and it also describes the relationship between the two poles. It forms a co-ordinated system that covers practically all phenomena of life and excludes nothing. Our Western systems, on the other hand, tend to cover one aspect of life in great detail, while leaving out the rest. The I Ching as we know it today may, here and there, be diluted by meaningless numerology; but the system itself is valid, as it says in the book's Great Appendix:

Yes, wide is the I Ching and great! If we speak of it in its farthest reaching, no limit can be set to it; if we speak of it with reference to what is near at hand, its lessons are still and correct; if we speak of it in connection with all between heaven and earth, it embraces all.

The I Ching functions like a great memory bank that is packed with the wisdom of the ages. But the most amazing computer is your own brain with its conscious and unconscious mind. When you connect your brain to the 'software' contained in your hexagram, it automatically selects the relevant clues out of millions of possible combinations. Your own mind becomes universal when it is inspired by a great teacher like the I Ching.

My final question was: 'Is the I Ching really so unique that it could never be duplicated?' I concluded that the book is indeed unique, but that a similar method could be developed. Various methods of divination have been known in the Far East since time immemorial. Some of these are quite simple and others more sophisticated. Of all these methods, the I Ching is undoubtedly the most comprehensive.

But all of them are based on the same principles. Many are practised to this day in Taiwan, Hong Kong, Singapore, Korea and Japan. I have consulted such 'oracles' in the temples of Taiwan and Japan several times – an enlightening experience each time. A Chinese friend showed me how it is done. After entering the temple, which is usually decorated with mystical dragons and other creatures, and filled with incense smoke, you bow to the spirit or god or goddess to whom it is dedicated. You clap your hands and pull a kind of cow bell 'to get the spirit's attention'. Now you formulate your question and say a little prayer. You take two half-moon shaped pieces of wood from a table, collect your mind and let the pieces fall to the floor. From the way they fall you know whether you have 'asked the right question and put it in the right way'. You restate your question if needed and proceed to a cylindrical container that holds about one hundred flat sticks, each about twenty inches long and numbered. You pull out one stick at random, all the time thinking of the question you would like to have answered. Then you give the stick to the caretaker, who reads the number and hands you a corresponding slip of paper. The vertical sequence of pictographs printed on the paper spells out your answer. It usually sounds very much like a condensed hexagram from the I Ching, or like some wise saying from Chinese literature, and it will seem relevant as soon as you relate it to the question you have asked.

After my trip to the Far East I experimented with this idea. I composed several dozen basic 'oracle answers' of my own by adding popular sayings to quotations from wise authors. These then served as my 'hexagrams' or answers. For instance, my Answer No. 16 would read: 'Grey is all theory and green the tree of life. A stitch in time saves nine. By displaying your wealth you

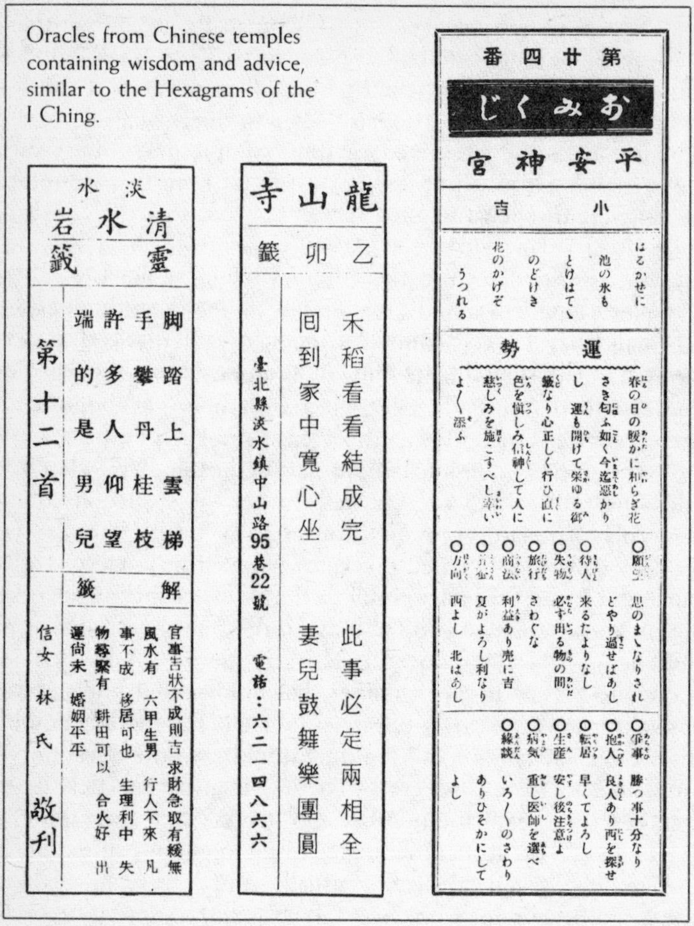

Oracles from Chinese temples
containing wisdom and advice,
similar to the Hexagrams of the
I Ching.

第廿四番

おみくじ

平安神宮

小　吉

はるかせに
池の水も
とけはてゝ
のどけき
花のかげぞ
うつれる

運　勢

春の日の長かに和らぎ花
さき匂ふ如く今迄悪かり
し運も開けて栄ゆる卸
愈なり心正しく行ひ直に
色を慎み付神して人に
慈しみを施こすべし喜い
よく運ふ

○願望	○待人	○失物	○旅行	○商法	○方向
思のまゝなりされ	来るたよりなし	蔵なり出る物の間に	さわなし	利益あり売に吉	万向
どやう過せばあし	良人あり西を探せ	必す出るなし		又がよろし利なり	西よし
					北はあし

○争事	○引越	○転居	○病気	○縁談	
膝つ半十分なり	早くてよろし	安し後注意よ	重し医師を選べ	いろ〳〵のさわり	よし
西を探せ	安し後注意よ			ありひそかにして	

淡水

岩　水清
籤　　靈

第十二首

脚踏上雲梯
手攀丹桂枝
許多人仰望
端的是男兒

籤　解

官事告狀不成則吉　求財念取有緩無
風水有　六甲生男　行人不來凡
事不成　移居可也　生理利中　失
物尋緊有　耕田可以　合火好
運命未　婚姻平平　出

信女　林氏

敬刊

龍山寺

乙卯籤

臺北縣淡水鎮中山路95巷22號

電話：六二一四八六六

禾稻看看結成完
囬到家中寬心坐

此事必定兩相全
妻兒鼓舞樂團圓

invite envy and robbery. Life is what you make it'. For
determining at random which answer applied at any given time I
used the following arbitrary system: I added the day's date to the
hour of the day and divided the total by two. In this way I let 'fate'
decide for me. The answers I got by this method were surprisingly
'accurate' and 'meaningful'.

This experiment proves to me that the human mind has the ability to select the right clues intuitively, even if it is confronted with an arbitrary selection of sayings and quotations. It tends to do the same when it faces a confusing situation in everyday life. Even the sight of a cup of tea-leaves or a constellation of stars will entice it to 'make sense' of the situation. It is our nature to search for meaning in everything we see.

Another explanation of the I Ching's effectiveness can be found in Lao Tzu's Tao Te Ching, another Chinese classic: 'Outside the Tao everything is wrong.' This implies that we can think and act right only after we have found the inner balance that is considered essential in all oriental teachings. As soon as we lose this harmony with the inner self and the cosmic powers, all aspects of our life are distorted. For example, our concept of past and future, body and mind, male and female, right and left, activity and rest is no longer in tune with life.

And because each of the sixty-four hexagrams in the I Ching discusses a different aspect of life, each one shows us how we can regain our balance in that particular area. Instead of problems we now begin to see solutions, and our thoughts and actions become more joyful and effective.

To illustrate this, some Chinese texts use the analogy of a central point surrounded by lines. As long as a person occupies this central position, he/she can look or move in any direction without obstruction. But whenever he gets off-centre, he can only move in two directions, his world becomes narrow, one-

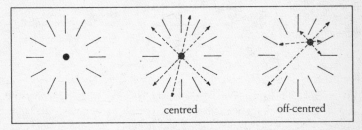

centred   off-centred

Centred and free to move in all directions.

Off-centre, therefore only able to move in one dimension.

dimensional and conflict-prone. He then tends to hurt himself and others in whatever he does and he keeps colliding with reality. By looking up his hexagram he can become aware of his one-sidedness and find his way back to the centre, the Tao, the 'Middle Path'. Once on the right track, all his thoughts and actions will become meaningful and effective again.

The virtue of the I Ching is that it gets us into a collected state of mind and then presents us with a balanced and wide-ranging selection of archetypal images mixed with practical wisdom. It offers an ingenious system for tapping our inherent creative and intuitive powers. To develop a comparable system should be possible, but it would amount to a huge project. If several hundred enlightened people would work at it over many generations, they would probably come up with a reasonable equivalent, or they might even surpass the original.

The next chapter will describe how our present version of the I Ching resulted from a co-operative effort involving hundreds of distinguished authors and spanning 5,000 years.

CHAPTER SEVEN

How the Book Evolved

Anciently, when King Fu Hsi had come to the rule of all under heaven, looking up, he contemplated the brilliant forms exhibited in the sky, and looking down he surveyed the patterns shown on earth. He contemplated the ornamental appearances of birds and beasts and the different suitabilities of the soil. Near at hand, in his own person, he found things for consideration, and the same at a distance, in things in general. On this he devised the eight trigrams, to show fully the attributes of the spirit-like and intelligent operations working secretly, and to classify the qualities of the myriads of things.

The basic concept of the I Ching was developed in China several thousand years ago, possibly around 3000 BC, when our own ancestors still had no culture to speak of. It seems that the Chinese have been a step ahead of us in many respects, as shown by some of their early inventions such as the compass, paper money, optical glasses and gunpowder. The book you have in front of you is another example of Chinese ingenuity. It was designed to help us understand the nature of life, and to work with the constantly changing forces that influence our inner and outer world. It is a practical book made by practical people, and the text refers often to questions relating to farming, hunting, travelling, social life, ethics, politics, warfare and various everyday activities. Although the picturesque language may sound puzzling to us at first, the underlying ideas are usually quite clear, even if a particular Chinese symbol may have several meanings. A single symbol can furthermore contain a whole story that must be translated in one or two English sentences. But in spite of all this it is possible to

'It is a practical book ... that refers often to questions about farming, hunting, travelling, social life ... and various everyday activities.'

express the gist of the ancient text in any language.

In the course of centuries, hundreds of great minds have added to this work. Much of the final text took shape about 3,000 years ago, and Confucius wrote extensive commentaries around the year 500 BC.

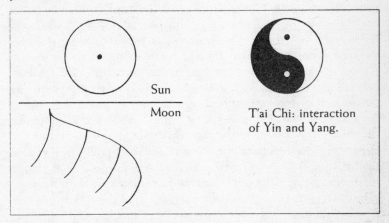

Sun

Moon

T'ai Chi: interaction of Yin and Yang.

The book's name, 'I Ching', as you may recall, means literally 'The System of Changes'. The pictorial symbol for 'I' (change) is composed of the symbol for the sun placed over that of the moon. The word 'Ching' refers to a grid-like system of co-ordinates, through which any point in space can be located and identified. Thus, the title describes the changing polarity between the light and the dark forces of life, between day and night, spirit and matter, body and mind, reason and intuition, heaven and earth, male and female. The same dynamic interplay is also expressed in the well known T'ai Chi emblem, where the dark half symbolizes Yin and the light half Yang. Each half also contains the seed of the other in the form of a black or a white dot.

As we have seen, both elements are equally important. There is no inherent contradiction between them, although the basic harmony between them can be disturbed at times.

If you are not familiar with the Far-Eastern mentality, it may take you a while to grasp the implications of this polarity in your everyday life. Are you now convinced, for example, that your mind is better than your body, that heaven is better than earth, that light is better than darkness? A Chinese would say that both poles depend on each other and are of equal significance. If one of them shows undesirable aspects, the complementing pole is bound to be equally out of balance. If Yin becomes too soft, this probably means that Yang has become too hard. If the wife is too domineering, the husband is probably too submissive. If the body is too sensuous, the mind is probably too rigid in some way.

The Far-Eastern ideal is therefore not so much to create the perfect mind or the perfect body, but to attain a harmonious balance between body and mind. Similarly, the aim is not to become a perfect man or a perfect woman, but to create a harmonious relationship between a man and a woman. Neither should we try to glorify the day (or the light or the sun) at the expense of the night (or the darkness or the moon). We should realize that both have their function and purpose, and that a harmonious cycle of night following day creates the right balance.

In the text, the short code for Yang is a solid line (——), while that for Yin is a broken line (— —). By arranging and multiplying the two lines in various ways, the ancient Chinese came up with countless combinations, each indicating a certain Yin–Yang polarity or stage of development. A Yin line on top of a Yang line, for instance, may indicate that a thing or person is soft outside and hard within. These combinations amount, in effect, to a sophisticated system of binary mathematics, as modern scientists are now finding out.

By combining three lines, eight sets of 'trigrams' are formed:

These trigrams are said to have been formulated and interpreted by the legendary King Fu Hsi more than 5,000 years ago.

They symbolized eight stages in the cycle of growth and decline, ebb and flow or appearance and disappearance that can be observed in all areas of life. The prime concern was at first with the seasons of the year and the cycles of the moon as they affected farming, fishing and hunting. Later it was found that the trigrams applied equally well to the changing thoughts and actions of individuals, and to social relationships, government and warfare.

Each trigram was then associated with certain images and attributes, depending on its position and area of application:

Attributes of the Eight Trigrams

chien
Active (Father)
Strong-willed, starting things, visible, lean.
Stallion, heaven, head.

kun
Devoted (Mother)
Gentle, patient, soft, dark, completing things, hidden.
Mare, cow, earth, heart.

chen
Arousing (Eldest Son)
Vehement, expanding, exciting, inciting.
Dragon, thunder.

sun
Gentle (Eldest Daughter)
Flexible, penetrating, gradual.
Chicken, wood, wind.

kan
Uncanny (Middle Son)
Threatening, deep, dangerous.
Boar, dangerous waters, abyss.

li
Graceful (Middle Daughter)
Brilliant, elegant, intelligent.
Pheasant, fire, lightning.

ken
Solid (Youngest Son)
Standing still, resting, arresting.
Dog, hills, mountains.

tui
Joyful (Youngest Daughter)
Pleasant, charming, satisfied, contented.
Sheep, lake.

At a much later date the trigrams were then combined with each other to form the 'hexagrams', which consist of six lines each. The sixty-four hexagrams were first interpreted by King Wen and the Duke of Chou about 3,000 years ago. At that time each hexagram text consisted only of one paragraph describing a particular human and cosmic situation, together with advice on how to handle it. This was the original structure of the I Ching, to which countless authors have added commentaries and refinements over the centuries. Thus the book as we know it today is a huge co-operative work spanning thousands of years and drawing on the collective creativity of China's foremost thinkers. The variety and universal, all-encompassing nature of the I Ching is partly due to this wealth of talent represented in it, and to the fact that the text keeps growing and maturing through the ages.

The sixty-four hexagrams are further amplified through several 'changing lines', which increase the total number of possible interpretations to over 10,000. In practice this means that you would hardly ever arrive at exactly the same hexagram twice, even in the space of many years.

Each hexagram contains favourable and unfavourable aspects, some lucky and some unlucky omens. You are made aware of a particular pattern of changes, of possible increase here and decrease there, of the continuous process of ebb and flow in all areas of your life, under the circumstances that prevail at the moment. You are shown how a 'noble sage' would handle your particular problem, and how a fool would make it worse. A wide range of human conditions, images, problems and solutions appears in each hexagram, together with references to the future and the past.

Even before the I Ching was developed, the Chinese used other, more primitive methods of asking for divine guidance. Divination was a matter of supreme importance to the rulers and sages of ancient China. They believed that the will of the gods or of the ancestors was made known through cracks produced by heating specially prepared bone and shell. Thousands of such pieces have recently been found by farmers while ploughing or

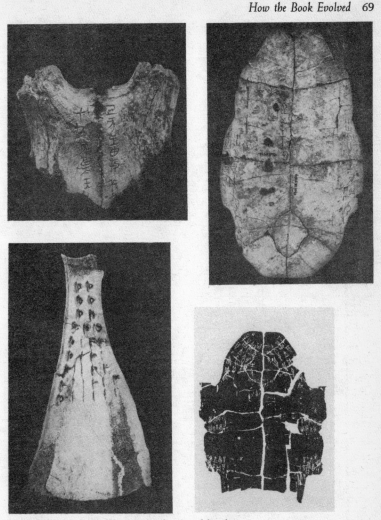

Inscribed turtle shell and cattle shoulder bone

after rain. These cattle shoulder bones and turtle shells were
inscribed with archaic pictographs, indicating the questions asked
and the answers received in the process of divination. Inscriptions
of this type are, in fact, the earliest written records of Chinese

'King Fu Hsi is credited with the invention of bows and arrows.'

history and the earliest known forms of Chinese writing.

The questions found on these oracle shells and bones cover a wide range of topics, including hunts, warfare, farming, building projects, travel, illness, the birth of children, the significance of dreams and various omens for the future. Here are some examples:

> 'Is the king's illness serious?'
> 'Should we use pitfall traps in the hunt?'
> 'Should the prisoners of the Chiang tribe be killed?'
> 'Will it rain tomorrow when we start our venture?'
> 'Will there be a rich wheat harvest?'

This simple method of asking for divine guidance served its purpose for many centuries, until the more sophisticated and comprehensive I Ching was developed and made known throughout the Far East.

Another interesting aspect of the I Ching is the description of King Fu Hsi's achievements 5,000 years ago, as related in the book's last chapter. Not only did this legendary ruler invent the trigrams on which the I Ching is based. He and his successors are also credited with introducing most of the basic elements of civilization in China. This description parallels to an amazing degree the findings of modern anthropologists and archaeologists. The sequence of inventions is related as follows:

> Invention of nets for hunting and fishing.
> Forming of wooden plough shares, and removing weeds.
> Holding markets for the exchange of products.
> Hollowing trees to make canoes, and forming oars.
> Using oxen and horses to pull carts.
> Building defensive gates and walls, and posting guards.
> Fashioning mortars and pestles to grind food.
> Invention of bows and arrows.
> Living in solid houses instead of in caves or in the open.
> Using written messages instead of knotted cords.

One of these written messages has, of course, come down to us in the form of the I Ching. Through countless generations, this book has had a profound influence on Chinese life and culture. Both Taoism and Confucianism have their roots in it, and have in turn contributed to it later. Confucius is said to have used his copy so often that the binding had to be replaced several times. Near the end of his life he said that, if he had another fifty years to live, he would dedicate them to the study of the I Ching. His contemporary Lao Tzu was said to have been inspired by this book to compose his famous Tao Te Ching, the classic of Taoism, of which over fifty translations have been published in a dozen languages.

The I Ching is the unquestioned 'Bible' of the Far East, together with the works of Confucius. Many Chinese, Japanese and Koreans turn to it for advice whenever they face important decisions in any area of life. Far-Eastern art, literature, medicine, politics and strategy are based on the concepts found in it. Even today's Red-Chinese believe that they can be happy and successful only if they follow these basic ideas that are ingrained in their culture, whether they admit it or not.

Most people who consult the I Ching today use the coin method described in Chapter 3. The ancient Chinese, however, used the more refined yarrow stalk method to obtain more meaningful and useful answers. The following chapter will tell you how you can apply this method that is part of the ancient tradition. Also explained is the pebble method, which forms a compromise between new and old methods.

Chapter Eight

Advanced Instructions

In this way, by consulting the yarrow stalks, we may receive an answer to our doubts, and we may also by means of them assist the spiritual power. ... He who knows the method of change and transformation may be said to know what is done by that spiritual power.

So far you have looked up your hexagrams by tossing the three coins, as described in Chapter 3. After you have used this simplified method to familiarize yourself with the book for some weeks or months, you can refine your approach and explore the deeper levels of the text. Although the coin method serves its purpose, it is somewhat unceremonious. Especially the use of common currency coins may give rise to mental associations that do not do justice to this ancient book.

To get into the proper frame of mind, the ancient Chinese used a complex method involving fifty yarrow stalks, which takes up to one hour for each consultation. They felt that this was a good investment of their time. Nothing was more important to them than to stay in tune with the cosmic cycles of change. Because they referred to the I Ching only occasionally and for really important matters, they spent only a very small fraction of their time consulting it.

The Pebble Method

Modern readers, who often feel that their time is limited, will find a suitable compromise in the pebble method, which takes a little

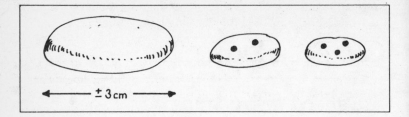

longer than the coin method but not as long as the yarrow stalk
method. For this you need only one pebble that is fairly flat on
both sides, more or less circular, about one inch in diameter, with
rounded edges. Take your time until you find one that you really
like and that you plan to keep for years. You will be surprised at
the wealth of beautiful pebbles you can find in your area, at the
beach, in a park, in the gravel of a nearby river or even in your
own garden. Appreciate the fact that this little marvel of nature is
millions of years old, perhaps billions of years. It has been shaped,
rounded and polished through the ages until it attained its present
form. It is truly a piece of eternity that puts you in touch with
elementary cosmic forces. Any physicist can tell you that it is a
microcosm of brimming, swirling electrons, as complex as the
millions of stars above you.

Next, mark one side of your pebble with two dots, the other
with three dots. This is easily done with a felt-tipped pen or with
paint. If you have chosen a dark pebble, mark it with a light
colour, such as the liquid white used to cover typing errors.
Finally, make a little pouch in which you keep your special stone,
out of red cloth or a similar material that appeals to you. Find a
place for it near the I Ching.

To obtain your hexagram with the pebble, proceed as you did
with the coins. But instead of throwing three coins once for each
line, you throw the one pebble three times. Shake the pebble
between your cupped hands for a few seconds. Then let it fall on
the table or a large flat surface. It will show either two dots or
three. Write down the result of the three throws. This total tells
you the number of the bottom line of your hexagram. If, for

example, you threw ⦂ + ⦙ + ⦂ , the total would be 7. Each total corresponds to a solid or broken line, as follows:

$$6 -\!\!- x \qquad 7 -\!\!\!- \qquad 8 -\!\!- \qquad 9 -\!\!\!- x$$

Therefore, the bottom line of your hexagram would in this case be a straight line (▬). Now continue building up the lines from the bottom up, by throwing the pebble three times for each line, and note the results. In all, you will have thrown the pebble eighteen times (3 × 6). Take your time and ponder over the question you would like to have answered while you keep adding the lines.

If a line is followed by an 'X', this means that it will change into its opposite, and you would interpret it as in the case of the coin method described in Chapter 3. In other words, the pebble method resembles the coin method in every respect, except that the throwing takes a little longer, which allows you to spend more time thinking about your question.

Whenever you are faced with a really decisive issue in your life, you will want to employ the ancient yarrow stalk method that is described at the end of this chapter. But whether you use coins, the pebble or the stalks, you will find that a certain amount of ceremony helps you to focus your mind and to obtain more relevant answers. The following list covers the essential points.

- Cultivate an atmosphere of quiet solitude while you consult the I Ching. Let members of your household or office staff know that you want to be alone for about half an hour. If necessary, hang a 'Do Not Disturb' sign outside your door and take the telephone receiver off the hook. Try to time your session during a quiet part of the day or late at night.
- Before starting the actual session, spend a few minutes just enjoying the silence. Leave the hustle and bustle of your everyday life behind. Loosen your belt, tie or dress, and take off your shoes if possible. Sit comfortably and relax all parts of your body, from the toes to the legs, the abdomen, the shoulders, the arms and hands, up to the face muscles. Your mind cannot let go of tensions and rigid thoughts as long as your body is still tense.

- Choose a posture that is relaxed but not slumping, so that your breath comes normally and spontaneously. Emphasize each out-breath to empty your lungs, and then let the air rush in by itself. Make sure that the air you breathe is as clean as possible.

- Align yourself with the greater scheme of things by becoming aware of your position in relation to the course of the sun, which rises in the east and sets in the west. Face north (toward the polar star) if you can conveniently do so. This is not essential, but it symbolizes your desire to harmonize with your natural and cosmic surroundings, which is also the basic purpose of the I Ching.

- Pull the curtains if possible, or use subdued lighting of a pleasant colour, or light one or two candles. Time your session in such a way that your mind is clear and you are not in a hurry. Your body should not be intoxicated or burdened by a heavy meal.

- By writing down your question you clarify your mind and become more aware of the real issue that concerns you deep down. When you look up your answer later, write down the gist of it in a few words, so that you can review it after the expected events have taken place. In retrospect you will discover additional revealing clues.

- Do the interpreting of your hexagram yourself – and do not try to interpret for others. The answer you get will always be highly subjective, and two people will see entirely different meanings in the same sentence or paragraph, depending on their present goals, circumstances and state of mind. If someone who is not familiar with the I Ching asks you to demonstrate it, let him/her throw the coins (pebble or stalks). Then look up the hexagram and let him read it by himself.

- Open your mind to the wider meaning of the text. Instead of taking words and sentences literally, discover their symbolic content and relate it to your particular circumstances. If the text says: 'Crossing the great water brings success', this does not mean that you should swim through the nearest river. Instead, it advises you to embark on a major venture.

- The I Ching was not designed to aid people in the pursuit of

'Before starting the actual session, spend a few minutes just enjoying the silence.'

selfish or destructive goals. It is not a success manual that shows how to get rich quick at other people's expense. Those who abuse the book with such purposes in mind are said to lose their access to the cosmic powers.

- You will find that each hexagram speaks about failure as well as success. This is so because no development can be entirely favourable or unfavourable. No situation can be entirely hopeless, and every victory brings its disappointments and unexpected traps. There are opportunities hidden in each failure, and some blessings come 'in disguise'. During times of chaos the forces of harmony gather strength. But when harmony is attained it cannot last and will sooner or later give way to tension and strife again. The purpose of the I Ching is to help us anticipate such changes, and to make the best of any given situation.
- You may consult the I Ching whenever you have a relevant question. But do not expect it to make all your decisions for you. This book is meant to enhance your mind, not to replace it. Use it with discretion.
- After each session, wrap the book in a cover or piece of cloth and keep it in a special place, together with the coins, the pebble and/or the yarrow stalks.

The Yarrow Stalk Method

For ceremonial purposes in ancient China, fifty yarrow stalks were used to arrive at a hexagram. The yarrow plant can be found in most areas of the world and is also known as milfoil. Its thin, hollow branches are straight and can conveniently be broken off into lengths of 4–6 inches. If this plant does not grow in your area, you may use other dry, straight stems of plants or straw, about 5 inches long.

Of the fifty stalks, one is put aside at the beginning of each session, so that in effect only forty-nine are used. To determine the bottom line of your hexagram, you would go through the following steps, and repeat the process for each succeeding line.

All other details are the same as in the coin and pebble method.

1. Find a quiet spot where you will not be disturbed. Relax and collect your mind for a few minutes. Formulate your question and write it down.
2. Divide the forty-nine stalks arbitrarily into two heaps.
3. Take one stalk from the right heap and put it between the last two fingers of your left hand.
4. Place the left heap into your left hand. With your right hand, begin removing four stalks at a time from your left hand, until only one, two, three or four stalks remain in this hand.
5. Place this remainder between your left middle finger and ring finger.
6. Next, place the right heap into your left hand and begin to remove four stalks at a time, until only one, two, three or four stalks remain, which you place between your left forefinger and middle finger.
7. Add up the stalks in your left hand. The total should be either nine or five.
8. The nine has the value of two, while the five is valued three (see box below).

Four stalks are valued	3	
Five stalks are valued	3	
Eight stalks are valued	2	
Nine stalks are valued	2	

9. Write down the value thus obtained, and put the nine or five stalks aside for the moment.
10. With the remaining stalks (forty or forty-four) you now repeat the process (see 1–9). Having written down the value obtained in this way, take what stalks are left, and repeat the process a final time.
11. By adding up the three values you have written down you determine the first line of your hexagram as with the coin or pebble method. Each total corresponds to a line as follows:

$$6 -- x \quad 7 — \quad 8 -- \quad 9 — x$$

12. This is the bottom line of your hexagram.
13. To arrive at the second line, you repeat the same process, starting with the full set of forty-nine stalks, as under No. 2 above.
14. Then you do it all over again for the remaining four lines, until you have built up all six lines of your hexagram. And remember that you build up from the bottom up, not from the top down.

As you can see, the procedure is quite involved, and the whole consultation will take up to one hour. But after the third or fourth time you will feel comfortable with the stalks and perform the counting more or less automatically. Once you have mastered the yarrow stalk method, you will find the results most rewarding.

PART TWO

The Sixty-Four Answers (Hexagrams)

(See also Index)

1. The Female Principle

The female principle, in its largeness, supports and contains all things. Its excellent capacity matches the power of the male principle. The various things obtain by it their full development.

This hexagram, made up of six soft lines, describes the Yin, the female life force of the universe. Its approach is down-to-earth and moderate, it pervades all things through gentle penetration rather than by overt force. It is symbolized by the mare, the beautiful and fertile animal that moves gracefully and is capable of great achievement.

The female principle is alive in all creatures and in every human being. Underneath our conscious everyday activities there is an unconscious power at work that sustains our efforts and brings about their completion, if we know how to co-operate with it. Without this Yin energy our thoughts and actions would be limited to a superficial level and we would accomplish little.

While the Yang, the male life force, tends to initiate developments through bold effort, the Yin usually accomplishes their gradual and natural completion. The Yin force is at work during quiet periods and during sleep, when it heals and rejuvenates the organism and gives it the new life energy that it needs during the day. Unlike the Yang force it tends to fulfill its vital function unobtrusively, without demanding attention and recognition. But it thrives on love and appreciation.

Because of its gentle and peaceful nature the Yin force can easily be swayed or hurt by external influences. Therefore it will sometimes need the protection and guidance of the Yang, the male principle (see Hexagram No. 2). The two forces complement each other, they normally form a harmonious union, although the harmony can be disturbed at times.

'The female principle, in its largeness, supports and contains all things. The various things obtain by it their full development.'

Changing Lines

Bottom Line When he notices hoar frost he knows that winter weather is not far off. Thus he moves cautiously and prepares for the quiet season, when he will have time to accumulate new life energy.

Second Line As long as he enjoys the support of nature, he will succeed almost without effort. Things will take shape of their own accord. There will be no need to initiate new projects at this point if he maintains his inner sincerity and firmness.

Third Line By working quietly and unobtrusively for a good cause, he reaps all the benefits of a good servant. By following a safe path or leader he avoids confusion and conflict.

Fourth Line During unfavourable times he withdraws and treads cautiously. Instead of wasting his resources on unprofitable projects, he rests and saves his energies for more promising days.

Fifth Line His quiet influence is felt all about him. Instead of showing off his powers, he quietly cultivates his inner qualities and allows them to permeate everything he does.

Top Line When he aggressively interferes where a gentle approach is called for, he will hurt others and himself. If he becomes impatient or fanatical he provokes opposition and defeats his purpose.

坤下　坤上

坤元亨利牝馬之貞　牝馬之貞　馬在下而行者也　牝馬順之所利　利牝

2. The Male Principle

The method of Khien is to change and transform, so that everything obtains its correct nature as appointed by the mind of Heaven, and great harmony is preserved in union.

The six straight lines of this hexagram indicate strength, energy and spiritual power originating in heaven. This male energy, also called Yang, balances the female Yin energy described in Hexagram No. 1. While the Yin nourishes all things and maintains a life-supporting environment, the Yang shapes the world in accordance with the cosmic order.

The Yang power is active within us and around us. During busy periods we can use it to initiate great projects, and in quiet times it can help us to build up our strength and develop our character. It gives our life meaning, direction and the creative spark. Without it we would vegetate and lose our initiative.

While the Yin approach tends to be patient, forgiving and down-to-earth, the Yang approach is more demanding and aggressive. In our daily life we need to make use of both approaches, just as we use two hands and walk on two legs. People who overstress either principle are using only half of their potential.

The male principle is capable of attaining great heights of creativity, power and fame. But when it loses touch with the moderating female principle, it soon becomes one-sided, arrogant or even brutal. In this way it often brings about its own downfall, and then seeks to blame this on the 'subversive' female or Yin influence.

During periods of rest the Yang energy will become dormant, while it recovers from previous exertions and gathers strength for coming challenges. This process of healing and rejuvenating is supported by the unobtrusive Yin influence.

東
君

'The male principle is more demanding and aggressive ... It is capable of attaining great heights of creativity, power and fame.'

乾乾
上下
乾元亨利貞初九潛龍勿用
〔乾〕文言備矣
蝎然反〔亨〕

Changing Lines

Bottom Line   If the time for action has not yet come, he prefers to stay in the background. He does not crave activity or attention for their own sake, but uses the quiet days to find himself and put his affairs in order.

Second Line   After a time of relative inactivity he can gradually begin to exert his influence, always keeping his purpose and his principles in mind.

Third Line   He uses his time creatively to get things underway and is busy all day. But in the evening he puts his worries aside and regains his inner balance.

Fourth Line   When he gets more involved and his projects begin to take off, he proceeds with care and remains true to himself.

Fifth Line   For a long time things were quiet, but there comes the day when the conditions are ripe for action and he can soar to great heights. By consulting an experienced and mature person he can avoid the danger of falling.

Top Line   While he ascends to new levels of influence and activity, he may be tempted to go to extremes and lose touch with the ground below. If he does not moderate his approach, he will isolate himself and provoke his downfall.

3. Difficult First Steps

The condition of the time is full of irregularities and obscurity.
... The superior man, in accordance with this, adjusts his
measures as in sorting the threads of the warp and woof.

In times of growth, plants struggle with difficulties out of
the earth, rising gradually above the surface. When
people embark on new ventures, they are not sure of
themselves at first. They often have to grope in the dark
while they explore new territory. Gradually they form a
mental concept of the situation, they adjust their
approach and consult with the people involved. Some of
the strangers they encounter may seem hostile at first. But
with most of them they will share common interests and
with some of them they will become friends later.

When a hunter advances into unfamiliar territory, he
can easily get lost and face serious difficulties. But by
consulting the resident forester first, he will find his way
and return with game. Similarly, in the beginning stages
of any project, it is advisable to advance intelligently and
to seek the counsel of those who are familiar with the
conditions.

A little favour at the right time will often win another
person's affection and smooth the way. But such gifts
should be tokens of appreciation and not obvious bribes.
They should be inconspicuous and of an appropriate
nature.

The growing process cannot be hurried, it must take
place in a natural, orderly manner. When people push
ahead with exaggerated expectations, they will be forced
to retreat and start all over again. They will then weep
and lament, but to no avail. The road is blocked and they
will not be able to advance until they have revised their
approach, consolidated their forces and formed a solid
base again.

坎下　艮上　蒙亨。匪我求童蒙，童蒙求我。初筮告，再三

畫江海
波濤法
山有奇
峯水亦
有奇峯
石尤怒
捲巨浪
排山海
月初溶
潮如白
馬是時
滿目皆
多崇岡
峻嶺吳
道玄畫
水終夜
有聲不
且善畫
縱畫水
風曹仁
希萬流

'The condition of the time is full of irregularities and obscurity.'

Changing Lines

Bottom Line When setting out on a new venture, he finds the situation unclear and confusing at first. He starts sorting things out. Without losing his dignity or his principles, he adjusts his approach, studies details and talks to everyone involved.

Second Line There are times when everything seems to fall apart and strangers intrude. But their intentions may not be bad. After careful consideration he may want to accept them as partners.

Third Line When he advances into unfamiliar territory, he will need the advice of those who live there. Without their help he would get lost and suffer serious defeat.

Fourth Line He encounters adverse conditions. But instead of pushing ahead independently, he uses his head and seeks the advice of experienced and sincere helpers. Thus he overcomes the obstacles and makes progress again.

Fifth Line Although he has much to offer and others expect him to be generous, he dispenses his favours with discretion. He gives inconspicuously and where help is deserved.

Top Line If he expects too much or has no clear plans, he will be forced to retreat, weeping and regretting. There is nothing else he can do then, until he withdraws to solid ground and finds the right approach.

艮上坎下

蒙亨匪我求童蒙童蒙求我初筮告再三

4. Learning and Teaching

The method of dealing with the young and ignorant is to nourish the correct nature belonging to them.

Life is a continuous learning process, and everybody is a student is some areas and a teacher in others. In any field of endeavour, some people are more experienced than others and can therefore share their experience. What is the best way of teaching and the best way of learning?

First of all, knowledge should be imparted in an orderly way so that the student does not get confused. But an overly structured approach would dampen the desire to learn and the ability to think creatively. All people have an inborn desire to improve themselves by learning about relevant aspects of life. This natural tendency is best brought out by an inspiring and understanding teacher who is an authority in his/her field but does not act like an authoritarian.

When people are forced to learn under the threat of punishment, as is the case in most schools, they memorize the material reluctantly and superficially, and they do not derive much benefit from it later. They cannot relate such dry knowledge to the everyday reality of their lives.

Instead of overwhelming the students with knowledge of this type, the teacher can encourage and elicit their questions, and stimulate their curiosity. In the optimal teaching situation the student approaches the teacher because he/she is eager to know certain things.

Such a situation exists when you, the reader, approach the I Ching with a relevant question. The more significant your question, the more significant will be the answer.

'Life is a continuous learning process, and everybody is a student in some areas and a teacher in others.'

坎震
上下
屯元
亨
利
貞
剛
故柔
屯始
乃交
大是
亨以
也屯
大也
亨不
則交
无則

Changing Lines

Bottom Line Just like a plant that follows a certain pattern when growing, a youthful or inexperienced mind needs guidance in its development. If the rules are clear and appropriate, corrections and rebukes will seldom be necessary.

Second Line Instead of using the authoritarian approach, he shares his experience like an equal and listens to suggestions from his students. He is kind to women and children.

Third Line He retains his dignity and self-respect when dealing with persons of influence or wealth. Accordingly he does not like to be worshipped by immature or inexperienced people.

Fourth Line Nobody can help those who insist on staying in their mental cages. Ignorant persons see only what they want to see and resent hearing the truth.

Fifth Line Those who are eager to learn and admit their inexperience will gladly be given advice. They are welcome anywhere and can easily find the right teacher.

Top Line Prevention is better than cure, and guiding a student wisely is better than punishing him after he makes a mistake. The better the teacher, the better the student.

5. Waiting

The superior man, in accordance with this, eats and drinks, feasts and enjoys himself as if there were nothing else to employ him.

The rain clouds come in their own time, bringing darkness but also the promise of a good harvest. Similarly we often find that approaching developments that look threatening from the distance may later turn out to be interesting challenges or opportunities. While the future takes shape there is usually not much we can do, and to interfere aggressively may only get us into trouble. There is no need to spoil our present enjoyment of life with worries about possible future events. As long as we are living from an inner core of strength and sincerity, we will be ready for any unforseen challenges. Only those who lack this inner core will suffer in anticipation and thus weaken themselves further.

Such quiet times are not wasted: they allow us to replenish our vital reserves, to rest up, to enjoy nourishing food and to remember our true purpose in life. Soon enough we will again get involved in struggles and conflicts that sap our energies and divert us from our path.

In the meantime we can appreciate our present blessings and any unexpected help that may come our way. Although our circumstances may not be ideal in every respect, we can now enjoy 'the little things that count' while we gather inner strength for unforeseen difficulties.

But as soon as we recognize an unavoidable emerging difficulty, we must adapt to the new situation and change our approach if necessary.

坎乾
上下
需
有孚光亨貞吉利涉大川。象曰需須也

'The superior man, in accordance with this, eats and drinks, feasts and enjoys himself as if there were nothing else to employ him.'

Changing Lines

Bottom Line His time will come if he keeps his purpose in mind. Taking bold action now may provoke opposition. It is better to wait at the sidelines until the time is ripe.

Second Line He waits in an open place where others may notice his weak spots and criticize him. But if he knows what he is doing, everything will turn out well in the end.

Third Line If he proceeds carelessly he will provoke opposition and invite his own injury. By adopting a more patient approach and keeping long-term goals in mind he avoids needless conflict.

Fourth Line Although he may already be in trouble, there is still time to adopt a more realistic approach that does justice to the circumstances.

Fifth Line After he has waited with firm correctness until the time is right, good fortune is on its way and there will be occasion to celebrate.

Top Line Just when he expects the worst and can see no way out, help can appear from an unexpected quarter and in an unexpected form. Although he has still not found the right place for himself, things turn out favourably.

坎上乾下。需。有孚光亨貞吉利涉大川。象曰需須也

6. Avoiding Conflict

The superior man, in accordance with this, in the transaction of affairs takes good counsel about his first steps.

乾坎
上下
訟。
有孚窒惕中吉。
可窒。謂窒塞也。能惕然後
以獲中吉。〔訟〕才用

Sometimes people get involved in conflicts, serious arguments or law suits even if they have the best intentions. Their first reaction may then be a feeling of rage and hate, and they may be tempted to hit back and fight to the bitter end. But by doing so they usually hurt themselves and they lose more than they gain.

The best policy in such cases is to weigh the alternatives calmly. First of all: is the argument worth getting excited about, or would it be better to forget it and to concentrate on more worthwhile things? Secondly: what are the chances of winning the case? It would be foolish to get into a fight that cannot be won. Thirdly: would the effort be worth it in terms of lost time, energy and peace of mind?

A further question is this: did we perhaps contribute to the conflict through our own unrealistic attitude? There may even be a chance that we provoked the whole incident through carelessness or preconceived ideas. By adopting a more constructive and suitable attitude we may change the whole constellation of events overnight and turn the situation to our favour.

But in any case it is advisable to tread carefully whenever we get entangled in such conflicts, to think the situation over calmly, and to seek the advice of an experienced and mature person where possible. An objective outsider can often see the cause of the trouble or act as a mediator.

'The superior man, in accordance with this, ... takes good counsel about his first steps.'

乾坎
上下
訟有
孚窒
惕中
吉

窒．謂
窒塞
也．能
惕．然
後

可
以
獲
中
吉
○
［訟］才
用

Changing Lines

Bottom Line Will it pay to pursue the matter to the bitter end? If the argument is not too serious, he prefers to ignore it. The gossip will soon die down if he pays no attention to it.

Second Line If his opponent has the obvious advantage, he cuts his losses and withdraws as diplomatically as possible. There is no disgrace in avoiding an otherwise certain defeat.

Third Line As long as he relies on proven allies and a safe base, he will avoid trouble. By staying in the shadow he avoids provoking attack.

Fourth Line He can avoid or remove some seemingly insurmountable obstructions by regaining his inner balance and vision. The solution becomes visible when he is no longer blinded by rage.

Fifth Line If a conflict is unavoidable, he can win in the end by using a balanced approach and by treading the narrow path between boldness and timidity.

Top Line Even though he may be in a position to win his case, some victories are not worth having because they cost too much in terms of wasted time, energy and nerves. And any gains he makes may soon be lost again if the circumstances are not in his favour.

7. Leadership

The superior man, in accordance with this, nourishes and educates the people, and he draws from them his support.

Organizations of all types are formed for the benefit of the members. Successful leaders inspire their followers and normally offer them a combination of protection and/or a livelihood, as in the case of armies and companies. The people, in turn, support the leadership, and thus the benefits are mutual. The same relationship also exists within each person, between mind and body, or between conscious and subconscious mind. Your conscious mind is the leader.

A good leader does not merely give orders; he/she familiarizes himself with the needs and problems of the people, and thus gains their respect and loyalty. Through his practical experience in the field he is in a position to make quick and realistic decisions and to execute orders from above.

An organization that allows incapable or inefficient people to rise to leading positions cannot thrive. The performance of all leaders must therefore be examined continuously, and organizational deadwood must be removed periodically. In this way the people will always have the feeling that the leadership can be trusted and that orders are given for good reasons.

Leaders need to remain flexible, so that the organization can adapt to changing conditions. By the same token the people need to limit their demands and give up some of their privileges during lean times. Losses, as well as profits, should be shared by all, and those who try to gain at the expense of the community must be punished. The leaders must see to it that such egoistic or negative influences do not take hold.

坤上坎下．師貞丈人吉无咎之丈正丈人嚴莊之稱乃吉也地與役師也

'A good leader does not merely give orders; he familiarizes himself with the needs and problems of the people.'

Changing Lines

Bottom Line If he makes the rules of conduct clear to all, there will be no confusion. He sees to it that the rules are appropriate.

Second Line The leader needs to be in touch with his people and join them in the collective effort. At the same time he follows the orders of the person or power above him.

Third Line He employs people in their proper places, so that all can perform their functions efficiently, and nobody has more power or influence than he/she deserves.

Fourth Line He runs a flexible organization that is equally ready to advance or retreat, depending on circumstances. Temporary withdrawal is no disgrace if the final goal is kept in mind.

Fifth Line He finds something to do for those who idly stray about, and he demotes those who hold positions beyond their capability. He also deals with other negative influences as soon as they crop up.

Top Line He delegates authority, but takes special care to promote only suitable and capable people. Those of weak character are given less influential positions.

坤上坎下 師 貞丈人吉无咎

之文正丈人乃吉

之文人嚴莊之稱也地為師

此也與役

8. Joining Together

坎坤
上下
比吉原筮元永貞无咎不寧方來後夫凶

Those who have not rest will come to him: high and low will respond.

Just as water has a natural tendency to flow towards the valley and collect in the lake, so people like to join together for mutual help and companionship.

But when you think of associating with others, be sure that you are guided by the right motives. Ask yourself if you have the right attitude towards them, and if they are your kind of people. Approach them with sincerity and take the proper steps when introducing yourself. If a friendship is to last, it must be based on complete openness and honesty, and the relationship must be spontaneous and voluntary on both sides.

When more people form a union, they need a focus, a central figure to hold them together. This must be a sincere person with unusual strength of character who enjoys the confidence of all. At the same time he/she should be humble and understanding, like the lake at the bottom of the valley to whom all rivers flow of their own accord. Such a social gathering point will also attract people who had been hesitant before, who had been waiting to make up their minds. But if they wait too long and do not join in time, they may find to their regret that they do not fit in later when the group has already found its form.

A group that is held together by mutual interest will have a beneficial effect on all members, and it will stay together without the need for persuasion or coercion, although it will adhere to certain basic rules of conduct. The members will feel privileged to volunteer for the various duties because they enjoy doing something worthwhile in worthwhile company.

'Just as water has a natural tendency to flow toward the valley and collect in a lake, so people like to join together for mutual help and companionship.'

坤上坎下

比

吉原筮元永貞无咎不寧方來後夫凶

Changing Lines

Bottom Line   When seeking to associate with others, he lets sincerity and loyalty be his guide. A union based on schemes and ulterior motives would be worthless or harmful.

Second Line   If a friendship does not allow for dignity and self-respect on both sides, it is not a real friendship. It is merely a union of people using each other for egotistical purposes, with all the accompanying pitfalls and frustrations.

Third Line   If he associates with the wrong people, he may prevent the right people from joining him. Therefore he limits his intimate relations to worthy persons, although he is polite and just to all.

Fourth Line   When seeking to associate with influential or more experienced persons, he pays them his respects without becoming submissive.

Fifth Line   The right associations form naturally and spontaneously, and it is worth waiting for them. Occasional solitude helps him to find himself while he keeps his eyes open for a genuine union.

Top Line   Friendship comes to those who are ready for it and who deserve it. By becoming a more sincere person and searching out the right places he will attract the right people.

9. The Restrained Approach

Hsiao Chu represents the symbols of strength and flexibility. ...
The superior man, in accordance with this, adorns the outward
manifestation of his virtue.

In normal everyday life it is the gentle, gradual approach
that brings the best results and avoids needless inner and
outer friction. Most of our projects need time, they
mature slowly, just like plants. By attempting to rush
them and to force quick or spectacular results we only
interfere with the natural process of evolution, we waste
energy and we may hurt ourselves.

Even though we may have the power and/or means to
push a project through, we are likely to antagonize
others, we swim against the tide and go against our own
inner nature. Without knowing it we resist our own
conscious plans and sabotage our own efforts.

If instead we take the comfortable, familiar path and
use friendly persuasion, the current of life will carry us
along. Although our achievements may not be instant or
spectacular, we will enjoy the support of nature, the
friendship of others and our inner peace. We will have
the needed time and leisure to enjoy the little things that
count and to cultivate our inner virtues. Sooner or later
our small achievements will add up and satisfy our desire
for success.

Such a congenial atmosphere inspires confidence in
others and encourages an attitude of mutual co-operation
and a spirit of community. People who trust each other in
this way have no need for great wealth, because they
know that they can depend on each other in times of
need. They also cultivate and maintain the inner strength
that may be required in emergencies.

巽上 乾下 小畜亨。不能畜大以亨。止健。剛志敢六志反敢密雲不雨。

'Most of our projects need time, they mature slowly, just like plants.'

Changing Lines

Bottom Line If he strays too far from the familiar paths, he will encounter danger and obstructions. Therefore he avoids needless adventures.

Second Line Those who get involved with too many people and projects will meet with difficulties and opposition. Therefore he prefers the company of compatible people and adheres to his accustomed way of life.

Third Line When there is friction and disagreement on basic issues, he moves and speaks with caution and does not attempt great changes.

Fourth Line Through his sincere attitude he inspires confidence and averts anxiety, suspicion and violence. Others feel a spontaneous desire to join his cause.

Fifth Line By cultivating his inner qualities he attracts others and enjoys their support, even though he may not be wealthy.

Top Line After achieving reasonable success he limits his aspirations and enjoys what he has. He does not invite failure through excessive demands.

巽上乾下。小畜亨。不能畜大止健。剛志故。密雲不雨。行。是以亨。○〔畜〕敕六反。

10. Treading with Caution

乾兑
上下
履虎
尾不
咥人
亨
象曰
履柔
履剛
也說
而

He treads on the tail of a tiger, which does not bite him. ... The superior man, in accordance with this, discriminates between high and low, and gives settlement to the aims of the people.

When dealing with different people, friction cannot always be avoided. But you will seldom step on other people's toes if your overall attitude is tactful and considerate. And if you do hurt their feelings accidentally, you will probably be forgiven. In any case it is a good idea to observe the rules of the game, to be aware of relationships and social positions and to be sensitive towards people's feelings. Many doors that are closed to clumsy and egocentric persons will be wide open to you if you are polite and well-mannered.

If your behaviour is pushy, for example, this creates counter-pressure, and others will try to put obstacles in your path – or at least they will withdraw their co-operation. And if you engage in gossip or intrigues, you will soon get caught in your own snares and prejudices.

Those who claim power and attention without deserving high positions will soon be humiliated, criticized and put into their place. Others who pursue their goals fanatically and ruthlessly will ignore obstacles, stumble over them and fall. Even those who try to do their best by paying close attention to small details will fail to see the wood for the trees and lose their main objective.

Thus, this hexagram shows us how to avoid needless friction by using our 'sixth sense' and by being aware of subtle differences in people and things.

'You will seldom step on other people's toes if your over-all attitude is tactful and considerate.'

乾兌
上下

履虎尾不咥人，亨。象曰、履柔履剛也，說而

Changing Lines

Bottom Line As long as he leads an unpretentious life and minds his own business, he can attain his cherished goals. By doing what he does well and by being useful he cannot fail.

Second Line By living quietly and keeping away from distractions, gossip and intrigue, he maintains his inner balance and avoids conflict.

Third Line Instead of claiming a high position and showing off, he remains where he belongs and where he is capable of performing a useful function.

Fourth Line If he has accidentally antagonized others, he hesitates and then moves on with extreme caution. Although he has stepped 'on the tiger's tail', he will not get hurt if he is tactful.

Fifth Line By pushing forward with too much determination he can easily hurt others and himself, he can overlook traps and dangers. Therefore he restores his inner balance and treads more carefully.

Top Line Instead of concentrating on the narrow details of the moment, he becomes aware of his entire project and the path that leads in many stages to his goal.

11. Harmony

The sage, in harmony with this, fashions and completes his regulations after the courses of heaven and earth, in order to benefit the people.

This hexagram shows three soft (Yin) lines resting on three firm (Yang) lines, thus indicating a harmony between the two primal cosmic forces: light and dark, heaven and earth, male and female. On the individual level this refers to the harmony between thoughts and feelings, conscious and subconscious, head and heart, mind and body, activity and rest, theory and practice, etc.

By cultivating such a happy balance within yourself you also create harmonious conditions around you. People of all types find it easier to co-operate with you. If you are in a leading position, your decisions will be more constructive and easily followed. And if you are in a learning position, your mind will be more receptive and eager to absorb information.

While in this state of inner harmony, you develop a new awareness, an ability to sense future developments, to see the consequences of certain ideas and events, and to act accordingly. You relate to others in a more subtle and sincere way. You also rely more on your inner resources and are not easily upset by outer events. By the same token you know who you are and do not base your self-esteem on your title, social position, possessions or inherited privileges. Your relationship with the opposite sex is less selfish and more loving and sincere.

Because you are firmly centred in yourself and harmonize with the cosmic order, you do not live in fear of times of turmoil that are bound to occur now and then.

'... A harmony between the two primal cosmic forces: light and dark, heaven and earth, male and female.'

Changing Lines

Bottom Line When his mind is centred, he becomes aware of the far-reaching consequences of his thoughts and actions, and of the hidden interconnections between people and events.

Second Line By cultivating a subtle inner harmony he is on good terms with people of all types, he can accomplish the most difficult tasks and he can perceive the most distant developments. He is guided by his inner light, not by outer pressure or obscure motives.

Third Line He keeps in mind that every plain is followed by mountains and that a state of harmony cannot last for ever. But by pursuing his goal and remaining firm he can enjoy the present and be ready for difficulties as they emerge.

Fourth Line If he relies too much on external aids and supports instead of his own inner strength, he will come down like an injured bird. Thus he heeds the warning and strengthens himself.

Fifth Line Instead of relying on accustomed or inherited privileges, he builds on the solid foundation of his own capabilities.

Top Line If he faces inevitable disarray or collapse, he realizes that heroic action would be futile. Therefore he withdraws and consults with his own people to avert the worst.

坤乾
上下
泰小往大來‘吉亨‘象曰‘泰小往大來吉亨‘

12. Disharmony

Heaven and earth are not communicating with each other. The superior man, in accordance with this, restrains the manifestation of his virtue and avoids the calamities that threaten him.

In this hexagram the lines are out of their proper order: three firm (Yang) lines rest on three soft (Yin) lines. Such a condition exists, for example, when the government is rigid and the people chaotic, or when a person has a rigid mind and chaotic feelings, or when a husband is arrogant and his wife devious. Each party then misunderstands and opposes the other, and disharmony pervails.

When you find yourself in such a situation, you can often locate the main cause of the trouble. By pulling out the main root you can then bring a whole complex of problems to the surface and deal with them one after the other.

But when this is not possible and the causes are beyond your control, you may just have to bear with it and pursue your goal calmly and unobtrusively. Do not let external disturbances unbalance you, refuse to get involved in other people's schemes and avoid panicking when others get nervous.

But there may be occasions when the general disharmony makes you feel confused and ashamed. Then it would not help to admit this to others. It is better to withdraw and create a new harmony within you and around you. By finding your own centre again you can also relate more harmoniously to others, and they will come to share your joy. Everything falls into place and you find your proper position in the cosmic scheme of things.

'The superior man, in accordance with this, restrains the manifestation of his virtue and avoids the calamities that threaten him.'

乾坤 上下 否之匪人。不利君子貞大往小來象曰否

Changing Lines

Bottom Line During periods of disharmony he faces a whole cluster of complex problems. But by pulling up the main root he can expose all related problems and deal with one after the other.

Second Line If he encounters obstacles and chaos, he does not react aggressively. Instead, he pursues his goal patiently and keeps a low profile. He maintains his inner firmness and does not panic like the others.

Third Line When he feels confused and ashamed, he does not show this. He withdraws and establishes a new inner and outer harmony. He evaluates his position and reconsiders his plans.

Fourth Line As soon as he harmonizes with the cosmic order, everything falls into place. His heart sings, and people come to share his joy.

Fifth Line Finally he begins to find the natural order again and he encounters fewer obstructions. But will he succeed? He guards against complacency.

Top Line There comes a time when the disruptive forces fade away, and a new harmony establishes itself naturally. He can then enjoy flowing with the general current of events.

13. Fellowship

The union of men appears here as simple as we find it in remote districts of the country. ... The superior man, in accordance with this, distinguishes things according to their kinds and classes.

People who share common interests tend to join and form groups. Such groups originate more or less spontaneously; they constitute simple fellowships rather than formal organizations.

Usually they start out with the best intentions of all involved. But disputes and jealousy can arise later, when it appears that certain factions or individuals are being favoured and that a spirit of clanishness is spreading.

Once such suspicions emerge, the members begin to fear each other, and they lose their spontaneity and become defensive or aggressive. This atmosphere of mistrust can last a very long time, unless the structure of the group is changed and a new start is made.

The animosity can go so far that some members consider taking the law into their own hands to get what they want, and the group is used as a vehicle for egotistical purposes. But after more arguing, screaming and fighting, they tend to come to their senses. They remember their common interests and forget their differences. With great relief they realize that the others are just as eager as they to make peace and enjoy the sincere fellowship they started out with.

乾離
上下
同人于野、亨、利涉大川、利君子貞象曰同

'They remember their common interests and forget their differences.'

Changing Lines

Bottom Line When people first come together, they usually have the most sincere intentions and display their best manners. He discriminates in the beginning to avoid arguments later.

Second Line When in a group, he will be tempted to favour his own people, which would create ill will and jealousy among the others. Therefore he remains impartial.

Third Line Once suspicion arises and the people begin to be afraid of each other, the union crumbles. It will take a very long time before mutual trust can be restored, unless the group is restructured.

Fourth Line He feels like attacking but hesitates. Just in time he realizes where this would lead him, and he decides to respect the law.

Fifth Line After many arguments and fights people can still find a common basis, they can discover the truth that unites them. Then they come together and laugh.

Top Line He joins others informally and without deeper commitment. There is no real union and not much loyalty is expected.

乾離
上下
同人于野、亨。利涉大川。利君子貞象曰同

14. Prosperity and Abundance

三三
離乾
上下
大有
元亨
乎
大大
有通
則何
必由
元得
亨大
夫有
象曰
大有

Ta Yu means a state of prosperity and abundance. ... The superior man, in accordance with this, discourages what is evil and gives distinction to what is good.

Possessions are a privilege but also a responsibility. Unless they are administered prudently they tend to disperse in time. This may not seem so obvious while you are still in the beginning stages of gathering wealth. But later you will discover that prosperity is no coincidence and that it has a tendency to disappear if it is not properly cared for.

First of all, it is not enough to guard your assets anxiously and to keep them where they are. They should be used creatively and in places where they are needed, and they should be used for a worthy cause. Possessions that are hoarded in a miserly spirit are a burden and exert a perverting influence, while a productive investment is a blessing to all involved.

In a way, you are not the exclusive owner of your wealth, and it is your duty to administer it for the benefit of the community as well as in your own interests. In any case you are only in charge of it while you are alive, and you will pass it on to those who come after you.

Although you will sometimes need the advice of experienced counsellors, you should have a clear idea of what you want. You need a goal and a strategy for your investments. Those who are swayed by rumours, dubious acquaintances or public opinion will see their wealth disappear. You owe it to your position to develop independent judgement and to maintain a certain reserve and dignity.

'Possessions are a privilege but also a responsibility.'

三三
離乾
上下
．
大有．
元亨．

㸒不
大大
有通
則何
必由
元得
亨大
矣有
．象
曰
大
有．

Changing Lines

Bottom Line While he is still beginning to gather wealth, not much can go wrong and possible losses will be small. But as he gets more prosperous he becomes aware of traps and difficulties.

Second Line He does not freeze his assets in one place but uses them where they are most productive.

Third Line Instead of hoarding his wealth like a miser, he uses it for a worthy cause and for the benefit of the community.

Fourth Line If he handles his wealth wisely and with discrimination, it will be preserved. He relies on the advice of experienced counsellors, not on rumours or public opinion.

Fifth Line In his relationships and dealings he is sincere and at the same time dignified. In this way others will not be tempted to impose on him.

Top Line He enjoys his prosperity as a gift from heaven and is grateful for the abundance of nature.

15. The Middle Way

The superior man, in accordance with this, diminishes what is excessive and increases where there is a deficiency, bringing about equality.

Nature favours a dynamic balance between Yin and Yang, heaven and earth, day and night, man and woman. Similarly, human beings tend to avoid excesses; they seek a natural balance between tension and relaxation, logic and intuition, thought and feeling, ideal and reality. The most desirable state lies in the middle between surplus and want, between excessive wealth and poverty, between total power and helplessness, between arrogance and servility.

Common sense and inner balance are prerequisites for success, and the successful person enhances his/her position and worth even more by remaining modest. Those who lose their balance and demand too much or too little of themselves or the world soon attract calamities and bring about their own failure.

By being aware of your own shortcomings and by striving to improve your inner qualities, you become the type of person who deserves and attracts luck or good fortune. Instead of trying to manipulate others, you let the forces of nature work in your favour. But at the same time you know what you want and you carry your projects through to their conclusion. You let people know that they can count on your sense of fair play, but that you expect the same of them.

You intend to be useful to others, but you do not let others exploit you. If people interpret your modesty and generosity as weakness and try to walk over you, you defend your legitimate rights and teach those a lesson who need one. At all times you walk the narrow path between arrogance and servility and maintain your inner balance.

艮上。坤下。謙亨。君子有終。象曰謙亨天道下濟而光

'Nature favours a dynamic balance between Yin and Yang, heaven and earth, day and night, man and woman.'

Changing Lines

Bottom Line He does not expect or claim too much or too little. He succeeds in matters great and small because his approach is moderate.

Second Line He practises moderation as a matter of principle, and lets others know that he treats them as equals and expects to be treated as an equal. People like his common sense and go along with him.

Third Line He knows what he wants and carries out his plans, without becoming pushy or rigid. Others join him because they like his simple, modest ways.

Fourth Line Without becoming submissive or servile, he is useful to others and earns their respect and reward. He is guided by common sense and looks neither down upon people nor up to them.

Fifth Line When someone tries to take advantage of his generosity he insists upon his rights, by using force if necessary. His neighbours will come to his aid even if he is not rich.

Top Line He keeps his own house in order and does not attempt to make the world over. He is aware of his weak areas and tries to improve his own qualities before attempting to correct the faults of others.

坤下
艮上
謙亨君子有終彖曰謙亨天道下濟而光

16.   Enjoyment

Yu denotes a condition of harmony and happy contentment. ...
The ancient kings, in accordance with this, composed their
music and did honour to virtue, presenting it especially and
most grandly to the gods and the ancestors.

People always yearn for harmonious conditions and inner contentment. They want to have a good time and enjoy life. But how can such a state be established and maintained? Or is it beyond our influence and dependent on mere luck and coincidence?

There is no doubt that, in the long run, the lucky ones are those who deserve to be lucky. Because they have a worthwhile goal in mind they are mentally prepared for opportunities and ready to make use of them. They anticipate the future and act accordingly in the present. Through their constructive attitude they radiate happiness and create harmonious conditions. Their enthusiasm attracts others and encourages them to co-operate and to see the best in each other. Even if they are afflicted by a permanent handicap, their enthusiastic attitude helps them to overcome or compensate for this.

In contrast to this are the people who believe that happiness is just a matter of luck, and that all they have to do is wait for it. Usually they wait in vain while they envy the 'lucky ones'. When they do stumble into favourable circumstances now and then, they naively boast of their luck and invite misfortune through their carelessness.

Then there are the people who short-change themselves by trying to find enjoyment in lowly and short-sighted pleasures that actually bring them more frustration than happiness. They lack the necessary enlightenment and purpose in life.

'People always yearn for harmonious conditions and inner contentment. They want to have a good time and enjoy life.'

Changing Lines

Bottom Line By showing off his good fortune he would invite calamity. Therefore he does not boast, and he enjoys his blessings quietly, without arousing envy.

Second Line If he looks ahead to anticipate future developments, and acts accordingly, all will be well. He does not wait until changes are forced upon him, but acts now.

Third Line If he passively looks up for favours while leading an easy life, he will be disappointed.

Fourth Line By creating harmonious conditions and acting with enthusiasm, he gathers friends around him and succeeds.

Fifth Line Even if he is plagued by a persistent complaint, his joyful attitude will carry him through.

Top Line He will not find enjoyment in life by pursuing lowly and short-sighted pleasures. True happiness will come to him when he develops a more enlightened attitude.

震上 坤下·豫·利建侯行師 彖曰豫剛應而志行順以

17. Following

Sui symbolizes the idea of following. ... The superior man, in accordance with this, when it is getting dark, enters his house and rests.

Just as night follows day, and winter follows summer, people follow the tides of life. They also follow their goals and ideals and their leaders, and they are in turn followed by others. Everybody is a leader in some ways and a follower in others.

By choosing meaningful guiding images and by associating with worthwhile people you can ensure your success in life. But if you spend your time in the company of fools and have no clear purpose in life, your energies will be wasted and you will lose your way.

Right now, for example, you may feel that it is time to change your priorities, to set new goals and to establish new relationships with worthwhile people. Your heart will tell you in which areas you need to make improvements.

If you want to be true to yourself and follow the right principles, you may have to leave some inferior habits and relationships behind, although these may seem important to you in your present state of mind. You will be surprised at the number of things to which you have become accustomed but which add nothing to your life.

After you find a new direction, people will sense the sincerity of your purpose, new relationships will form and some people may want to join your cause. Others, however, will leave you because they feel offended by your honest approach. It would not be worth your while to hold them through compromises and flattery. As long as you are sincerely committed to the right values, everything else in your life will fall into place.

'The superior man, in accordance with this, when it is getting dark, enters his house and rests.'

Changing Lines

Bottom Line   If he really wants to be true to himself, he may have to associate with different people and change his goal in life. By going about this in the right way he can ensure his success.

Second Line   As long as he associates with immature people, he will not be considered worthy of good company.

Third Line   He begins to find more worthwhile company and lets go of superficial or foolish relationships. While he is looking, he uses his solitude to come to terms with himself.

Fourth Line   If he gains followers through flattery and ulterior motives, this may satisfy his ego for a while. But by thus sacrificing his principles he will harvest inner and outer conflict.

Fifth Line   By following a meaningful goal and adhering to worthy principles, he awakens his creative energies and attains what he wants.

Top Line   As long as he is sincerely committed to the right values and cultivates worthwhile relationships, nothing can harm him, and all minor issues will take care of themselves.

兌震
上下

隨元亨利貞。无咎。象曰隨剛來而下柔動

18. Revising Obsolete Patterns

The end of confusion is the beginning of order; such is the procedure of Heaven. The superior man, in accordance with this, helps the people and nourishes his own virtue.

To a great extent our life is determined by our past: by habits, customs and traditions. Some of these we have created ourselves and others we have adopted or inherited.

Such patterns are convenient to follow, they relieve us of many needless decisions. On the other hand we must realize that they can become traps and ruts which lead into stagnation and decay. As conditions change, established patterns must be revised. We must not allow them to become ends in themselves, we must subordinate them to our main goal in life.

Some of these patterns are more rigid and demanding, as if imposed by a fatherly authority or by a set mind. Others are more soft and indulgent, as if introduced by a motherly authority or by an understanding heart. In both cases it would be futile to attempt a radical break with the past. As is well known, even subtle everyday habits have a way of fiercely resisting change. A more intelligent approach is called for here, that takes into account the deeper root causes and hidden motives. In this way it becomes possible to satisfy the underlying (justified) need in a more appropriate way, and to find a new order.

Neither the individual nor society would be able to function without habits and customs, which are both regulated by the subconscious mind. Our purpose is not to defeat the unconscious, but to create a new harmony between its automatic way of doing things and the innovative ways of the conscious mind, so that we become the masters of our fate and not the slaves of the past.

'To a great extent our life is determined by our past: by habits, customs and traditions.'

艮上 巽下 蠱 元亨利涉大川先甲三日後甲三日 象

Changing Lines

Bottom Line If he blindly follows the accustomed or traditional path, he inherits the faults together with the virtues of the past.

Second Line Instead of going along with easy and self-indulgent ways of doing things he gently restores the balance and introduces a new order.

Third Line If he is faced with rigid habits or demanding traditions, he knows that it would be futile to revolt against them. Instead, he proceeds with subtlety and intelligence to replace the obsolete order with a more appropriate one.

Fourth Line If he accepts indulgently the easy-going patterns set up in the past, he will end up in humiliating circumstances. Therefore he establishes higher standards.

Fifth Line He reviews the obsolete standards and creates a new order. If he handles the situation intelligently, he will be praised by all involved.

Top Line Instead of adhering to the accustomed way of life followed by others, he decides to be his own master and to follow his own conscience.

19. Gathering Strength

There will be great progress and success, while it will be advantageous to be firmly correct.

The Lin hexagram describes how a person achieves success and advances to a position of influence. Slowly at first, the development gathers strength, then culminates and brings with it the danger of decline and downfall. A premature decline can be avoided by establishing firm and honest principles right from the beginning.

Once you have attained a high position, you may be tempted to accumulate more and more power, and to neglect other fields of endeavour. This would provoke resistance and envy, and disturb your own inner balance. Instead, you should now begin to share your know-how and wisdom, to delegate authority and promote self-government. In this way, others will be proud to serve you and they will not be tempted to undermine your position. They will, in fact, want to support you because they know that they benefit from your experience and wise counsel.

During a time of increasing influence and strength you will want to make the best of the many opportunities that come your way. But through easy success you may be tempted to become complacent and to neglect your principles and inner virtues. Remember that your advance grew out of humble beginnings and that it cannot last for ever. If you rely too much on outer success for your self-esteem, your ego may often be deflated through external obstacles over which you have no control. The real source of your strength lies within you, in your harmony with the cosmic powers. You owe your success to this core of strength, and you can rely on it in times of outer adversity.

'The real source of your strength lies within you, in your harmony with the cosmic powers.'

Changing Lines

Bottom Line He begins to find support among others, and his own confidence grows. Like-minded people join him, and they move ahead together. At this stage he asks himself if he is moving in the right direction and if his advance is guided by intelligence.

Second Line When he is on his way towards the goal, he asks himself if it is the right goal. He remembers that his progress will run into obstacles now and then, and that it cannot last for ever.

Third Line When things are going well he will be tempted to become complacent and he may lose his inner conviction. But all will be well if he maintains a degree of self-discipline and the proper firmness in his dealings with others.

Fourth Line After he has succeeded and reached a position of influence, he does not monopolize his power. He works constructively with others, sharing his know-how with them, thus ensuring their support.

Fifth Line Once he has attained an influential or leading position, he uses his power wisely. He delegates authority to the right people and promotes self-government. In this way he avoids envy and needless power struggle, and everybody feels that he performs an important function.

Top Line When he has reached the desired position, he sets an example for others by being honest and generous. He becomes known as a wise person who gladly shares his wisdom and helps deserving people.

兑下
坤上

臨元亨利貞至于八月有凶,象曰臨剛浸

20. Deep Understanding

☰☷

巽坤
上下
觀盥而不薦有孚顒若王道之宗廟之可觀者莫之莫

Kuan shows the sage with sincerity and an appearance of dignity. All beneath look to him and are transformed.

A person who occupies a high vantage point has a wide horizon and is at the same time exposed to the view of those below. If you have attained a deeper understanding of life, people expect you to behave in a mature and dignified way. They sense that you have access to certain worthwhile insights, and unconsciously they try to learn from you. By the same token you know of persons whom you consider wise and who serve you as examples.

In our everyday life we often look merely at the surface, tending to miss the wider significance of things. We are busily rushing from one subject to the next, without taking the time to contemplate the deeper aspects. Instead of going out and taking a closer look, we tend to stay home, judge things from the distance and maintain our narrow point of view.

We tend to be so preoccupied with details that we forget the meaning of life and our own progress over the years. Only in rare moments we remember that we are in the process of realizing a vision, a glorious dream. By relating today's issues to the course of our entire life we can suddenly become aware of their deeper significance. At the same time we remember to orient ourselves to our main goal in life and to our role in the cosmic scheme of things.

'A person who occupies a high vantage point has a wide horizon and is at the same time exposed to the view of those below.'

Changing Lines

Bottom Line   Has he understood the situation, or is he merely looking at the surface? He contemplates the issue more thoroughly, like a mature person.

Second Line   If he merely looks at the issue from the distance, his conclusions will be limited by his narrow point of view.

Third Line   By taking his whole life into consideration, he gets a better perspective of things.

Fourth Line   Instead of looking at small matters, he maintains an awareness of his great dream, his glorious vision of life.

Fifth Line   Today's events are no coincidence. They are the result of his past actions and they will, in turn, influence his future.

Top Line   Instead of looking only at his selfish little aims, he relates his life to the greater scheme of things.

巽坤
上下

觀盥而不薦有孚顒若王道之可觀者莫
盛乎宗廟觀宗廟之莫

21. Biting Through

Union by means of biting through the intervening article: The ancient kings, in accordance with this, framed their penalties with intelligence and promulgated their laws.

Harmonious conditions can at times arrive spontaneously and naturally. But at other times they have to be brought about by forceful action, by 'biting through' an obstruction.

If in a society certain people ignore the laws followed by others, they have to be punished, and the laws must have 'teeth'. In the same way the individual must be willing to practise a certain degree of self-discipline in order to attain the desired inner harmony or the union with the self. Life has its own laws to which we are all subject. Whoever breaks them must suffer the consequences. In a way we are all our own judges, executioners and gaolers, and we even build our own mental cages.

When people err only slightly or for the first time, the punishment need only be light and symbolic, so that they can easily get back on the right track. But in the case of premeditated and repeated violations, tougher measures are in order. The judge then needs to be very careful to maintain impartiality and a sense of justice. All too easily he/she can sink to the level of the sinner and become vengeful and violent himself.

This applies also to people who try to break with their own bad habits or unnatural desires: they will only succeed if they look at themselves objectively and set reasonable goals. Through needless self-castigation and self-condemnation they would only anchor their problems more firmly in their minds. They achieve more by recognizing the underlying need and finding the proper outlet for it.

'The ancient kings framed their penalties with intelligence and promulgated their laws.'

Changing Lines

Bottom Line   If this is the first time he errs, he will get away with a mild penalty. If there were no bad intentions and he can easily mend his ways, a rebuke may be sufficient.

Second Line   In the case of a slight deviation he need not clamp down too hard, as long as the point has been made.

Third Line   If he encounters a nasty obstruction, he needs to watch out so that he does not get hurt. He also needs to make sure that his own position is proper and that he is not acting outside his authority or power.

Fourth Line   Now and then he will meet with a really tough obstacle or opponent which needs to be handled with equally tough and straightforward measures. If his mind is clear and decisive, he will succeed.

Fifth Line   When he needs to enforce justified demands in a difficult case, he should be aware of his perilous position and maintain his impartiality.

Top Line   If he stubbornly pursues his dubious course and does not listen to wise counsel or his own conscience, he will provoke inner and outer conflicts.

離震
上下

噬嗑亨利用獄

噬嗑
齧也
噬嗑合也
頤中有物
曰噬嗑
物之不齊
由飲

22. Ornament

As there is ornament in nature, so shall there be in society. But its place is secondary to that of what is substantial.

People have a natural hunger for beauty. They like nice surroundings, good-looking partners, appealing clothes, elegant entertainment and polished labour-saving devices. When they feel that their life is becoming a sober and boring routine, they usually try to replace the missing element by adding surface ornamentation. They hope that life will regain its former beauty if they acquire a shiny new vehicle, fashionable clothes, a supply of intoxicating beverages, or if they start a new love affair.

But while all these things can add a nice touch to an otherwise contented life, they cannot create happiness in themselves, and the sense of novelty soon wears off. True happiness originates within a person, in the deeper levels of being, through the harmony with the inner self and the cosmic order.

When people and things possess this innate harmony between form and content, they are naturally beautiful and do not require additional adornment. Plants and flowers, for example, are beautiful because they are 'elegant solutions' of Nature: their forms and colours are functional. The same is true of really well-designed and functional tools and buildings. And people who harmonize with their inner nature and perform a meaningful function in life will radiate beauty even in their work clothes.

By the same token people can entertain each other with pleasant and amusing conversation. But when projects have to get done and important decisions have to be made, a more practical approach is called for.

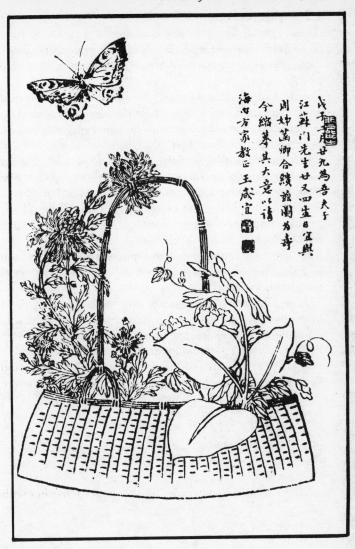

'As there is ornament in nature, so shall there be in society. But its place is secondary to that of what is substantial.'

Changing Lines

Bottom Line If he takes the conveniences of civilization too much for granted, he will become their slave. Although vehicles can be useful, he prefers to walk where possible.

Second Line Although he cares about his phyiscal appearance and his clothes, his self-esteem is not based on these things. He relies more on his inner qualities and on right thoughts and actions.

Third Line He likes to have a good time and enjoy a social drink now and then, but this does not divert him from his everyday tasks and his main goal in life.

Fourth Line Although he enjoys an occasional flirt, he is mainly interested in a more substantial and lasting relationship with the opposite sex.

Fifth Line He appreciates the poetic side of life and beautiful surroundings, but his basic attitude is practical and down-to-earth.

Top Line Instead of trying to beautify things with external ornaments, he prefers the simple and functional forms. In other people he appreciates simplicity and sincerity.

離上
艮下

賁亨小利有攸往。

彖曰賁亨柔來而文剛。

23. Unstable Foundations

The superior man, in accordance with this, seeks to strengthen those below him, to secure the peace and stability of his own position.

This hexagram shows one firm (Yang) line resting on a foundation of five soft (Yin) lines. Such a one-sided arrangement can bring danger, but it also offers opportunities. If the soft element gains further, it could undermine the solitary Yang element and cause its downfall. But if the Yang force is guided by strong and honest principles, it will enjoy the support of the Yin, and in this way both elements will benefit.

Such circumstances can arise when a person has strong emotions or a big heart (Yin), but lacks reason and proper guiding principles (Yang). A similar imbalance could also exist in families where the female (Yin) element greatly outweighs the male (Yang) element, or in organizations with emotional leaders. In each case the balance can either be regained – or it can be totally lost.

For example, if your life is dominated by vague feelings and obscure emotions, your thoughts and actions will tend to be unreasonable and emotional, and things might eventually get completely out of hand. But if you adopt a more realistic attitude and learn to guide your emotional energies into constructive channels, the balance will be restored. You will be swept to success through the sheer power of your vital (Yin) forces.

The same applies to the relationship between management and staff or government and people: weak or arrogant leaders will be overthrown, but reasonable leaders with honest principles will enjoy the support of the people whom they guide towards mutual success.

艮坤
上下
剝不利有攸往
象曰剝剝也柔變剛也不

'Reasonable leaders with honest principles will enjoy the support of the people whom they guide toward mutual success.'

Changing Lines

Bottom Line If his attitude is weak or arrogant, his position will be undermined and his project will collapse, as if he were lying on a bed with weak legs. He can strengthen his base by adopting a more realistic attitude.

Second Line When he sees the decline coming and still does not abandon his unrealistic attitude, he will be overthrown and lose everything.

Third Line He realizes that the old must go to make room for the new. He revises his approach, helps to dismantle an obsolete order and looks at the world with new eyes.

Fourth Line After the foundation has crumbled, he can still save his skin if he faces the truth and starts again on solid ground. But if he does not drop his illusions, he will suffer serious injury.

Fifth Line As soon as he drops obsolete ideas and is guided by the right principles, he will regain his self-confidence, and others will follow him like a school of fish.

Top Line After the balance is re-established between thoughts and emotions, between man and woman, and between Yin and Yang, everything falls into place and the destructive elements disappear.

艮下　坤上　剝　不利有攸往。象曰　剝剝也　柔變剛也　不

24. The Turning Point

Change is the law of nature and society. When decay has reached its climax, recovery will begin to take place.

The Fu hexagram shows the light (Yang) element gaining and the dark (Yin) element receding. After a long night the sun is rising again. The period of rest or stagnation is coming to an end, and it is time to wake up and get busy. Fu can also symbolize the recovery from a period of decay.

Cyclical changes are the rule in nature and in the lives of people, and by understanding them we can work with them instead of against them. We can anticipate the turning points and do the proper thing at the proper time. In this way we are sure that we get the needed rest after a time of activity – and that we are bright and full of energy when the busy period begins again. We can also choose to let things take their own course for a while and then take charge again to channel events in the right direction.

The pattern of waves, vibrations and cycles fulfils an important function everywhere in nature, in society and in the life of the individual. These movements are normally moderate and harmonious, they do not swing from one extreme to the other. They form an even rhythm of up and down, back and forth, coming and going. Accordingly it is best to seek an even rhythm between activity and rest or between departure and return, and to avoid extremes.

But turbulent periods do occur now and then, and the person who adheres to his/her goal and who knows how to steer the middle course will benefit most in the changing fortunes of life.

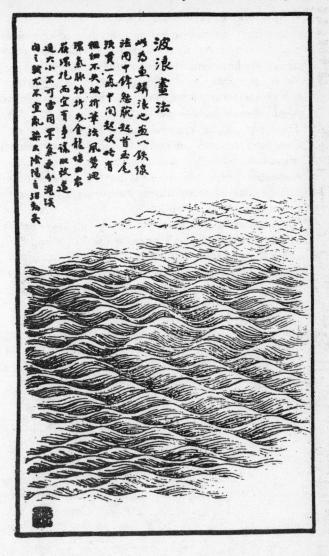

'The pattern of waves, vibrations and cycles fulfills an important function everywhere in nature, in society and in the life of the individual.'

坤下 震上 復 亨 出入无疾 朋來无咎 反復其道 七日

Changing Lines

Bottom Line Instead of letting the cycle of change swing from one extreme to the other, he soon returns to the happy medium and maintains his balance.

Second Line By quietly following the trend of the times he lets things return to normal, and by doing so earns the admiration of the others.

Third Line If he changes his course often and lacks direction, he will manoeuvre himself into dangerous situations.

Fourth Line Even when he has started out with others, it may be wise to return alone, if the company turns out to be unsuitable.

Fifth Line If he maintains his dignity and inner balance in turbulent times, he will ride out the storm and have no cause for regret.

Top Line If he misunderstands the signals of change and misses the turning point, everything will go wrong and he will not recover for a long time.

25. Innocent Success

Can anything be done advantageously by him whom the will and appointment of Heaven do not help?

This hexagram describes a stage of innocence that brings success and 'good luck' spontaneously. While you are in this state of harmony with yourself and the cosmic powers, everything you do seems to turn out to everybody's advantage. You receive benefits from all sides, people enjoy helping you and you often reap where you did not previously sow.

But whenever you lose this inner sincerity, the opposite happens: everything you do seems to work against you, even the best plans and intentions go wrong, people suspect your motives, and the fruit of your efforts is spoilt. In such circumstances it is usually best to abstain from all action temporarily and to scrutinize your deeper feelings: are you free of all ulterior motives, hidden hostility or tendencies to twist the truth? Now is the time to rediscover the innocence of the heart with which all people are born but which they tend to lose later. In this state you will once more communicate with the forces of nature that can support your needs and make your dreams possible.

Even illness cannot harm you while you maintain this innocent attitude, and you soon recover without the use of medicine. If people see their own ulterior motives in you and accuse you without justification, this cannot hurt you either. Your reputation may suffer temporarily, but this will not affect your happiness. Your self-esteem is not primarily based on the opinion of others, it grows out of a firm inner conviction that your thoughts and actions harmonize with the cosmic order. Although you like to live in harmony with others, your first obligation is to the voice of your heart that tells you what is right.

'In this state you will once more communicate with the forces of nature that can support your needs and make your dreams come true.'

Changing Lines

Bottom Line As long as he is free from insincerity and listens to the subtle voice of his heart, everything will turn out right.

Second Line When his intentions are innocent, he will attain his desires without effort. He will enjoy the support of nature and often reap without sowing, by benefiting from the abundance of creation.

Third Line If others misunderstand and accuse him, this will not hurt him as long as his heart is pure and as long as he knows that he is not at fault. He perseveres in what he is doing, without resenting those who oppose him.

Fourth Line External obstacles cannot upset him as long as he is firmly convinced that what he is doing is right. Obstructions will soon disappear if he perseveres with a pure heart.

Fifth Line Even illness cannot harm him while he harmonizes with nature and his own nature. There is no need to take medicine, which may only interfere with the healing process. He will recover spontaneously.

Top Line But even if his heart is free of insincerity he does not count on his luck for ever. There will be periods in his life when it is necessary to limit expectations and plans, and to wait until the time is ripe for further action.

乾震
上下

无妄元亨利貞其匪正有眚不利有攸往。

26.   The Power of Knowledge

The superior man, in accordance with this, stores largely in his memory the words and deeds of former men, to subserve the accumulation of his virtue.

The Ta Chu hexagram shows us how to make good use of acquired knowledge and of our own mental faculties. Through science and culture we have access to enormous stores of accumulated know-how, and through continued practice we can become masters in the use of this reservoir of experience.

But there is the danger that we may use these powers recklessly or for the wrong purposes. We must remember that science is meant to be a servant and not a master, and that it can be beneficial only when used by enlightened people for worthy causes. This is why the above quotation states that 'the words and deeds of former men' ought to be subservient to 'the accumulation of virtue'.

Furthermore, knowledge can only be useful if it is structured around a worthy central theme, so that all details make sense in the greater context. The mere accumulation of book knowledge, on the other hand, would only burden the mind instead of enhancing it. Many an 'educated' person is less able to deal with life than the peasant who never went to school.

The human mind has an almost unlimited potential for the good or for the bad. It needs to be used with great respect and subtlety. We can fully enjoy its blessings only if we first harmonize with the cosmic powers.

'He stores in his memory the words and deeds of former men, to subserve the accumulation of his virtue.'

Changing Lines

Bottom Line Instead of using his knowledge recklessly or indiscriminately, he waits until he has found a worthy cause.

Second Line If he cannot find a central idea around which the details can arrange themselves, his movements will be blocked.

Third Line With continued practice and a careful attitude he can develop the mental power that will bring success in every respect.

Fourth Line Instead of using his mental powers ruthlessly like a bull, he proceeds with intelligence along the path of least resistance.

Fifth Line Even when he has to deal with crude forces or opponents, he disarms them through his intelligent approach.

Top Line When he becomes a true master of his mental faculties, he will enjoy the support of nature and his own unconscious mind, and all obstacles will disappear.

艮上乾下　大畜　利貞不家食吉利涉大川　象曰大畜

27. Seeking Nourishment

We must look at what we are seeking to nourish, and by the exercise of our thoughts seek for the proper aliment.

Heaven and earth nourish all things, and human beings form part of this cosmic arrangement. We seek to nourish ourselves and those we love, and we cultivate and encourage the things and ideas that we consider worthwhile. As long as we nourish the right things in the right way, we prosper.

Everybody needs a source of income and makes his living in his own way. Those who seek support from the wrong sources or for the wrong reasons will go hungry and feel like beggars.

Nourishing food need not be fancy or expensive. The healthiest ingredients are usually found nearby, and they are plentiful and inexpensive. Fancy foods from faraway places tend to be less wholesome. If we develop a craving for them we may satisfy the palate but starve the body, or we may envy those who can afford them. Everything we need is contained in the food that nature provides, and by refining it too much we reduce its value.

When we nourish those whom we love and who deserve our support, we can wholeheartedly pursue this unselfish goal, like a 'hungry tiger'. But to obtain enough food we need not succeed in a big way. Persistent and sustained effort usually serves the purpose best. We owe it to those who depend on us to plan wisely and to provide a continuous supply of nourishment. By taking food on a regular basis we allow body and mind to function more efficiently than under a feast-and-famine diet.

'We must look at what we are seeking to nourish, and by the exercise of our thoughts seek for the proper aliment.'

Changing Lines

Bottom Line By living simply he will have enough to nourish himself and not go hungry. But if he develops expensive tastes and envies others, he will suffer.

Second Line As long as he depends on his proper source of nourishment, all is well. But if he fails to obtain a living in this way and seeks support from strangers, he will go hungry.

Third Line If he fails to eat the right things or if he nourishes himself in the wrong way, he will lose his vital energy. He will be too weak for effective action until he recovers through proper food.

Fourth Line He is strongly motivated by an unselfish desire to provide nourishment for others. Like a hungry tiger he pursues his aim and succeeds.

Fifth Line To find sufficient nourishment it is not necessary to engage in gigantic projects. Modest but steady effort will provide enough for all.

Top Line Those who provide nourishment for others must plan in a prudent and responsible way; they cannot depend on good luck or the mercy of others.

艮上 震下 頤。貞吉。觀頤。自求口實象曰頤貞吉養正

28. Inner Strength

Great indeed is the work to be done in this very extraordinary time. The superior man, in accordance with this, stands up alone and has no fear.

People can thrive even under extraordinary circumstances if they have the necessary inner strength. In tense times they can brace themselves and remain masters of the situation. But they need to be aware of their perilous position and proceed with great caution in everything they do. If they push ahead recklessly they may go beyond the breaking point. Once this happens, the damage may have been done and even their best friends cannot rescue them.

But by using a more cautious approach they can avoid all this and make the best of prevailing circumstances. Even when the situation seems stagnant or hopeless, they will have the inner strength to initiate a renewal and to plant for a new harvest.

To succeed in this they have to plant in fertile soil, their projects must be based on solid foundations. They must be confident and able to win the support of their neighbours.

As long as their thoughts are merely theoretical and not based on experience and practical considerations, their projects will stand on weak feet and collapse under pressure. If their conscious effort is not supported by heart-felt convictions and faith, it will not stand up to the stresses that are bound to develop now and then. To succeed under extraordinary circumstances, people must be able to 'stand up alone and have no fear', as the above quotation states. Even though these qualities may not be needed in the normal everyday routine, and even though there is usually no need to exhibit them, they are prerequisites for survival in the long term.

'They will have the inner strength to initiate a renewal and to plant for a new harvest.'

Changing Lines

Bottom Line When faced with extraordinary circumstances, he takes all necessary precautions to avoid damage. Once damage has been done, he may not be able to repair it.

Second Line Even if the circumstances seem stagnant or hopeless, he knows that a person's inner strength makes renewal possible.

Third Line If he pushes on beyond the breaking point, the damage will be serious, and nobody will be able to help him.

Fourth Line Instead of bending under pressure, he braces himself and remains master of the situation.

Fifth Line Exhausted soil cannot produce strong plants. Therefore he makes sure that he has the necessary confidence, that he has support from below and that his projects have a solid foundation.

Top Line When he has to ford a stream or when he starts on an important new venture, he makes sure that the water will not go above his head.

兌巽
上下
大過。
之音相
過．過
棟橈利有攸往亨象曰大過

29. The Dangerous Ravine

The superior man, in accordance with this, maintains constantly the virtue of his heart and the integrity of his conduct, and instructs with simple words.

Danger is here symbolized by a wild stream rushing through a deep ravine. In such surroundings, people can easily fall on sharp rocks or drown in the current. But by adopting a careful attitude, such dangers can be avoided.

If, after the initial scare, people get used to the danger and become careless, they may get into serious trouble. Therefore they must constantly be aware of the fact that one wrong step is enough to undo all their previous efforts. Only by proceeding intelligently, step by step, and by choosing the path of least resistance, can they avoid the perils that threaten everywhere.

There will be moments in your life when you feel that you are entirely surrounded by danger and that there is no escape. No matter where you go or look, your path seems to be blocked. If you then panic and try to struggle free, you will only entangle yourself further. All you can do in such a situation is relax, collect yourself and look at the alternatives calmly. Most likely you will then find that in your confusion you overlooked one perfectly acceptable route of escape – or else you will have to wait a little until the circumstances change in your favour.

In dangerous times you will have no use for luxuries, conveniences and long conversations. Simple meals and short words will serve the purpose. And above all you will need a flexible mind and the ability to learn quickly from experience.

雲流泉斷法
畫泉古人多用雲鎖然
畫雲時不可露出筆蹟
痕跡但以顏色輕輕漬
出方為妙手

'Danger is here symbolized by a wild stream rushing through a deep ravine.'

Changing Lines

Bottom Line After he has faced the same danger many times, he may get used to it and become careless.

Second Line If he finds himself in dangerous circumstances, he will be tempted to push his way through, instead of moving cautiously, step by step to avoid accidents.

Third Line If he is surrounded by danger on all sides, any desperate action on his part would only make the situation worse. Therefore he clears his mind and waits until the circumstances change in his favour.

Fourth Line While he is threatened by danger, simple food and drink in earthen vessels will serve the purpose. Simple words will suffice to convey urgent messages when time is short.

Fifth Line When the time of relief seems to be near, he watches developments and postpones decisions or new ventures.

Top Line If he feels that he is completely trapped and bound by external circumstances, he can free himself by adopting a more flexible attitude and by abandoning his preconceived ideas.

坎下坎上習坎之坎・險陷之名也・習謂便

〔坎〕苦〔便〕婢面反・有孚維心

之・〇〔坎〕苦・習絡反便習謂便習

30.   Gentle Clarity

The great man, in accordance with this, cultivates more and more his brilliant virtue and diffuses its brightness over the four quarters of the land.

The Li hexagram is symbolized by a clinging flame. It shows us how we can illuminate the world around us by cultivating our inner clarity. While a confused and obscure mind sees only confusing superficial appearances, the clear mind sees the hidden meaning and the cosmic life force in everything. While the confused person tries to feel young and alive by living it up in wild extremes, the enlightened person lives naturally and permanently in harmony with life.

When you are guided by this gentle inner light, undesirable external influences have no power over you and cannot distract you from your main purpose in life. You also have no fear of death or ageing because you consider yourself a part of the cosmos. You accept the cosmic cycle of day and night, waking and sleeping, life and death, as natural and necessary.

When you encounter people who lack this gentle clarity, who put on a noisy show of self-importance, you will sense the frustration and desperation behind their façade. Such people live in a hell of their own making, stewing in their own juice. Although a heaven on earth is within their reach, they have forgotten how to follow their inner guiding light. They flutter like moths around some external light and get burned again and again, until finally they give up and abandon their illusions. They will then be ready to ascend to a more enlightened level of consciousness, where they can distinguish between life-supporting and life-destroying influences.

'We can illuminate the world around us by cultivating our inner clarity.'

離 離
上 下

離利貞亨

而 離
後 之
乃 為
亨 卦
故 以
曰 柔
利 為
貞 正
亨 故
也 必
· 貞

畜

Changing Lines

Bottom Line If he is confused and lacks mental focus, he will be tossed around by external forces. By composing himself he gains the inner clarity that leads to a more desirable way of life.

Second Line By cultivating his inner balance and avoiding extremes he makes good use of the prevailing circumstances and finds happiness.

Third Line Some people try to feel young by living it up. Others moan about their approaching old age. But the enlightened person always feels alive deep down and has no fear.

Fourth Line Hectic and noisy behaviour brings frustration and accidents. By maintaining his gentle inner clarity he can turn his life into heaven on earth.

Fifth Line If he sees his worldly hopes vanishing, he will weep and despair. But after his illusions have died he will be reborn with a clearer mind, ready to enjoy a more enlightened life.

Top Line Instead of condemning or idealizing things and people, he calmly distinguishes between good and bad qualities in each case. By weeding out undesirable elements or by rearranging them he creates a new harmony.

31. Mutual Influence

Heaven and earth exert their influence, and there ensue the transformation and production of all things. The superior man, in accordance with this, keeps his mind free from preoccupation and open to receive the influences of others.

People influence each other in varying degrees and on different levels. In the relationship between husband and wife we see the most basic and vivid example of mutual influence. But a similar interaction also takes place within each person, between the head and the heart, between the conscious and unconscious minds. And each individual is constantly interacting with neighbours, friends, relatives and colleagues at work in the course of daily life.

To really reach and motivate people, we have to appeal to their hearts and satisfy their intellects at the same time. Mere talk will leave others cold; it will not arouse their emotions. They would feel more deeply touched by the non-verbal appeal of an affectionate dog than by their neighbour's chatter that registers only in their intellect.

To influence others we also have to be fully convinced ourselves. If our message does not come from the heart or if our heart is not in our project, others will sense this and decline to go along. If we present ideas that have not been fully thought through or tested in practice, we will only convey our own uncertainty to our listeners. Even though we may be eager to share our half-baked visions with them, it is better to control this impulse until they are fully matured.

Finally it is worth remembering that all influence is mutual. Our hearts should be open to the justified appeals of others, and we should be ready to abandon any preconceived or ego-centred ideas.

'In the relationship between husband and wife we see the most basic and vivid example of mutual influence.'

Changing Lines

Bottom Line If he merely has a subtle hunch and is not yet convinced of his idea, he will not be able to convince others either.

Second Line Even if he feels fairly certain that he ought to act, he should not yet try to get others to join him until he settles things in his heart.

Third Line Instead of trying to influence anybody and everybody, he controls this impulse and gets involved with a few worthy people.

Fourth Line He asks himself if his heart is in his project. If he is not really sure of his intentions, others will sense this and decline to go along. Only his closest friends will follow him.

Fifth Line A forceful approach will impress some people. But others would resent this attempt to influence them, preferring a more subtle appeal.

Top Line If he appeals only to the intellect of people by overwhelming them with a flood of abstract words, they may agree with them on the surface, but they will not be truly moved.

兌下。艮上。咸亨利貞。取女吉象曰咸感也柔上而剛

32.   Perseverance

When we look at what they continue doing long, the natural tendencies of heaven, earth and all things can be seen. The superior man, in accordance with this, stands firm and does not change his method of operation.

The secret of nature is patience and perseverance. Similarly, success is usually the result of persistent effort. When someone seemingly succeeds 'overnight', a closer look reveals a background of extensive preparation. Not much can be accomplished without long practice and a certain amount of routine.

The same is true of relationships between people. A lasting and beneficial bond between a man and a woman rests inevitably on a firm commitment to proven values and on persistent efforts on both sides. But while the woman tends to fulfil her function by following the pattern set by tradition and guiding principles, the man must also initiate new patterns when this is required by changing external conditions.

Any changes of the established routine must be introduced cautiously and gradually. New ideas must first be tested to ensure their suitability, and they must be applied in a flexible way. A rigid imposition of changes would provoke sabotage or revolt. The same is true on the individual level, when obsolete habits have to be changed: the unconscious mind will adopt new habits only if it can be convinced of an urgent need, and if the transition is made gradually.

While perseverance is a prerequisite to success, it is no end in itself, and it should serve a worthy goal. The hunter who searches in the wrong places or for the wrong game must fail in spite of his perseverance. Similarly it would be foolish for him to keep hunting when he has no real need for additional game.

'The secret of nature is patience and perseverance. Similarly, success is usually the result of persistent effort.'

Changing Lines

Bottom Line   In the beginning he needs to be flexible. If he formulates his methods and goals too soon, they will not suit the conditions and lead to failure.

Second Line   As long as he perseveres in harmony with the laws of nature, he has nothing to worry about and everything will turn out well.

Third Line   He needs to pursue his goal. But if he does not cultivate his inner firmness, he will be at the mercy of changing moods and external influences.

Fourth Line   Perseverance will not help if the hunter searches for game in the wrong places. He needs intelligence as well.

Fifth Line   There are two types of perseverance: the Yin (female) approach relies on tradition and diplomacy, while the Yang (male) approach initiates new patterns to deal with changing external conditions.

Top Line   If he keeps persisting after the need for perseverance has gone, he will only waste his energies and resources.

震 巽
上 下
恆
亨
无
咎
利
貞

恆 而
道 亨
亨 以
乃 濟
无 三
咎 事
也 恆
恆 恆
通 之
无
為
遜

33.   Retreat

Great indeed is the significance of the time that necessitates retiring. The superior man, in accordance with this, keeps small men at a distance, not by showing that he hates them, but by his own dignified gravity.

During the day the sun shines, but in the evening it disappears, the moon takes over and the dark element dominates. During active (Yang) periods we advance, expand and spend energy, and during restful (Yin) periods we retreat and allow new life energy to accumulate.

By understanding these cycles of change we can time our movements to coincide with the trends of life. For example, there are times that call for expansion and progress. But there are also times when we need to consolidate our position and simplify our way of life. If we do this intelligently and gracefully, we maintain our inner strength, and we can turn a potential defeat into a victory.

When we first notice that our progress has come to an end for the present, we may be shocked and afraid. We may lose our self-confidence or feel ashamed, especially if others are looking on. But retreating is part of life, it is an art that can be learned like any other art. We may, for instance, simply ignore the difficulties and go on calmly with our task until things change to our favour. Or we may quietly and with dignity move on to solid ground. Or we may simplify our way of life by doing without some luxuries and by limiting our emotional involvements.

But to retreat gracefully we need to have inner strength and we need to remain masters of the situation. In this way we are not being pushed back, but we are swinging with the natural cycle of advance and retreat.

乾下艮上．遯亨．小利貞。象曰。遯亨。遯而亨也。義．遯之乃爲

'During restful (Yin) periods we retreat and allow new life energy to accumulate.'

Changing Lines

Bottom Line Instead of withdrawing in fear and panic, he calmly moves to safe ground and maintains his dignity.

Second Line If he firmly persists in his moderate ways, few people will have the power to make him retreat.

Third Line If he listens too much to others, he will no longer be master of the situation. Emotional ties will hinder his efforts to simplify his life.

Fourth Line A person of strong character can afford to give some ground without losing face, while a weak person would feel disgraced and become afraid or violent.

Fifth Line If he sees the change coming, he can still find a diplomatic solution that allows him to depart as a friend, without hard feelings.

Top Line If he is above the situation and emotionally detached, he can retreat gracefully, without a sense of loss.

乾上
艮下

遯亨。小利貞。象曰。遯亨。遯而亨也。

義．遯之爲

遯
乃爲

34.　Gentle Strength

震上　乾下

大壯利貞。象曰大壯大者壯也。爻。大者謂陽小者道將

*Strength should be held in subordination to the idea of right,
and exerted only in harmony with it. ... The superior man, in
accordance with this, does not take a step which is not
according to propriety.*

This hexagram shows four hard (Yang) lines underneath
two soft (Yin) lines, indicating dynamic power led by
gentleness. In all areas of life, happiness and success
depend on the harmony between these two elements: in
the relationship between man and woman, parents and
children, management and staff. On the individual level
we have to balance our will-power with our conscience,
our intellect with our intuition.

To accomplish anything in life, we need an abundant
supply of vital life energy. This energy flows from
unconscious sources, it is a gift of nature, But to make the
best of it we must use it with subtlety and intelligence,
and in accordance with our conscience that tells us what
is right. Instead of pushing ahead clumsily and
impulsively like a ram, we can use this power efficiently.
Instead of applying it indiscriminately from our
periphery, we can direct it from the subtle centre of our
being and achieve spectacular results with a minimum of
effort.

In this way we never have to exhaust our vitality in
desperate efforts, and we always have plenty of energy
left for emergencies. On the other hand we must be ready
to throw our full weight behind a worthy cause when
necessary. While the gentle approach is suitable in
normal circumstances, there are moments in life when a
dynamic push is called for.

虎色圖

利劍不可近美人不可親
利劍近傷手美人近傷
身遠險不生處十步呼擭
輪情愛不在多一夕防傷神

唐寅

'Dynamic power led by gentleness: to make the best of our strength we must use it with subtlety and intelligence.'

震乾
上下

大壯利貞象曰大壯大者壯也

爻 大者謂陽

小者道將

Changing Lines

Bottom Line If he moves clumsily and impulsively, without thinking, he will exhaust his energies and cause accidents.

Second Line By acting from his centre and with firm conviction, he overcomes resistance and succeeds. But he needs to guard against unwarranted enthusiasm and over-confidence.

Third Line By using all his energies in desperate efforts, like a ram, he would exhaust himself and have no reserves left for emergencies.

Fourth Line Power is concentrated in the axle of a wheel, not along its rim. Thus he succeeds by acting from the centre of his being, not from his periphery.

Fifth Line During easy times he will not need to exert himself or use force. His strength will be dormant. But in the end he may forget how to use it in difficult times.

Top Line There are times when dynamic action would accomplish nothing and where active interference would only complicate matters. But by becoming aware of the difficulties and using his head he can find a way out.

35. Advance

The superior man, according to this, gives himself to make more brilliant his bright virtue.

This hexagram explains how a person can best get ahead in life, and how he/she can overcome obstacles and avoid pitfalls. As the quotation above points out, the main secret of successs is 'to give yourself', to render a useful service or to join a worthy cause. By advancing with suitable allies towards a common goal, everybody benefits and 'makes his bright virtue more brilliant'. Although it may sometimes be necessary to move on alone, without the support of like-minded companions, such attempts are usually more laborious and less successful.

Secondly, the goal that is pursued alone or with others should be worthwhile and meaningful. It should be approached with sincerity and patience from the very beginning. A hasty attitude or an attempt to get ahead by shady means would only retard the progress.

On any path there will be some expected setbacks and gains of a minor nature. These should be taken in one's stride, without worrying or rejoicing. They should not be allowed to divert the attention from the main goal. By steadfastly staying on the right path, the advance will be rapid and the outcome will be worthwhile.

But if a major obstacle should emerge, a forceful effort may be needed to clear the way. This may involve some friction and frustration. The present approach or attitude may prove inadequate and a new one may have to be found to get things underway again. In any case it is best to proceed cautiously and moderately, and to maintain faith and confidence in the project.

'The main secret of success is 'to give yourself', to render a useful service or to join a worthy cause.'

Changing Lines

Bottom Line At first his advance is slow and he is on his own. But he is on the right path, and through his generous and sincere attitude he will soon gain the confidence of others.

Second Line Things seem to go well, but yet he is not happy. If he perseveres patiently his sorrow will disappear. His moderate approach finds the approval of his gentle grandmother or a well-meaning supporter.

Third Line As soon as the others trust him, he can advance with them towards a common goal. Obstacles are more easily overcome by joint action.

Fourth Line If he advances shrewdly and uses dubious ways of getting ahead, his schemes will eventually be exposed and he will be caught like a rat.

Fifth Line As long as he is on the right path he need not worry about temporary changes of fortune. He can move ahead confidently and concentrate on the main goal. What counts is the end result.

Top Line He can avoid most obstacles by proceeding cautiously and by continuously correcting his own approach. But when a major obstacle blocks his path, he may have to use force to remove it. This may involve some friction and frustration, but all will be well in the end.

離上 坤下 晉 康侯用錫馬蕃庶晝日三接 象曰 晉進

36. Hiding the Light

It will be advantageous to realize the difficulty of the situation. The superior man, in accordance with this, conducts his management of men; he shows his intelligence by obscuring it.

When the sun shines, birds spread their wings, they rise to heaven and sing. But when storm-clouds gather, they find a safe hiding place close to earth and pull in their wings. In the same way people show their bright sides and enjoy recognition during favourable times. But when the tide turns against them, they pull in their horns and return to a more modest way of life.

Whenever you enter a dark period in your life, you will want to come down to earth and reduce your expenditures. By keeping a low profile you can avoid accidents and escape the attention of potential opponents. Try to blend in with the crowd and do not show others how bright or successful you are. Pay no attention to gossip or jealous remarks. Pursue your goals quietly and do not bite off more than you can chew. Hire help if you feel that a task is beyond your strength.

Above all, remember your main purpose and follow your inner light. Even though you do not show your light to others, you always need to be aware of it yourself. It will enable you to persevere under difficult circumstances and it will give you inner strength even in your darkest hours. You will emerge from such dark periods with a strengthened and purified character if you remain true to your ideal. Thus you will never really lose control even though you may temporarily be caught in an inferior position.

'When storm clouds gather, birds find a safe hiding place close to earth and pull in their wings.'

坤離
上下

明夷利艱貞象曰明入地中明夷內文明

Changing Lines

Bottom Line   In difficult times he keeps a low profile. He does not arouse envy or opposition by showing off. Quietly he goes about his business, does not take on new tasks and ignores the gossip and rumours around him.

Second Line   When things turn for the worse and his mobility is limited, he engages the aid of a strong helper.

Third Line   By pursuing his goal in a flexible way he can gain control again. But complete order cannot be restored at once.

Fourth Line   Even in his darkest hour he can still follow his inner light and move imperceptibly towards his goal.

Fifth Line   If he finds himself caught in an inferior position, he can still get his way by hiding his light and persevering unnoticed.

Top Line   When he notices that the time of his glory is coming to an end, he faces the facts, comes down to earth and adopts a more modest way of life.

37. A Household

Bring the family to that state of harmony and all under heaven will be established.

Households, families and organizations need a certain inner structure to bring out the best in each member and in the unit as a whole. Some members attend more to external matters, such as earning an income, while others take care of internal matters, such as ensuring good health and preparing food. Some members are more experienced in certain fields and fulfil a teaching or leading role, while others prepare themselves for future roles by helping and by learning in the process.

In the family, for instance, the father usually deals more with the outer world and makes decisions that concern external matters. The mother creates a life-supporting atmosphere within the family and sets the general tone. She enriches the family life through her love and inner harmony; she prepares nourishing meals and balances income and expenses. The older children assist their parents and prepare themselves for their future parental role, while the younger children learn to exercise their developing faculties by playing and by imitating the more experienced members of the family.

Thus, everybody has his or her function and contributes to the whole. The co-operative enterprise thrives through mutual love and is regulated by certain rules of conduct. These rules need to harmonize with human nature, so that they are practised naturally and joyfully. They should be understood by all and applied in a reasonable way, without needless severity.

When families function smoothly in this way, the entire society enjoys peace and prosperity. Under such conditions there is no fertile soil for violence, insanity or perversity. All organizations, great and small, can then structure themselves according to the example of the 'happy family', with each member fulfilling his or her function in the scheme of things.

巽離
上下．
家人利女貞。

家人之義，各自脩一家之道．不能知家外他人之事也，統．

'Thus, everybody has his or her function and contributes to the whole.'

Changing Lines

Bottom Line   He helps to establish a certain basic structure within the community, before confusion arises through overlapping duties. Improper habits may be hard to correct later.

Second Line   When he gets involved with internal community affairs, he proceeds with tact and patience, by using the female or motherly approach. The internal needs, such as health, comfort and nourishment usually require someone's undivided attention.

Third Line   When emotions are allowed to run wild, regret soon follows. Harsh words spoken in anger can do irreparable damage. Uncontrolled silliness and diversion usually lead to sadness and humiliation. But he can find a healthy balance between chaos on the one hand and needless control or severity on the other.

Fourth Line   One member ensures the prosperity of the community by watching the budget, by planning income and expenses. When the treasurer (or the mother) plans with prudence, there will be no emergencies and the household will thrive.

Fifth Line   Good parents or leaders are respected but not feared. They create an atmosphere of mutual love and direct the communal affairs for the benefit of all. They encourage the best in each member through their constructive attitude and strength of character.

Top Line   If the father acts with inner conviction and is guided by firm principles of truth, he will enjoy the respect of all. In any community, the leader needs to be inspired by high principles of a reasonable and practical nature.

38.   Misunderstanding

上下 離兑

睽 小 事 吉 彖 曰 睽 火 動 而 上 澤 動 而 下 二

Male and female are separate and apart, but with a commomn will they seek the same object. There is diversity between the myriad classes of beings, but there is an analogy between their several operations. The superior man, in accordance with this, where there is a general agreement, yet admits diversity.

Two poles oppose each other, but at the same time they form one whole and complement each other: north and south, day and night, light and dark, above and below, before and after, yes and no, sweet and sour, male and female, thoughts and feelings. Everywhere in nature we can see such polarized pairs of opposites that simultaneously attract and repel each other.

In the same way people who really belong together can sometimes misunderstand each other. Or enemies can be strangely bound to each other, disliking and yet needing each other.

But when you are involved in an argument with people who are really your kind, they will eventually find back to you spontaneously and without effort on your part. By the same token you will have no luck if you seek friendship with people who are not your kind, and such people will also try in vain to make friends with you. Birds of a feather flock together because they share a common background. And opposites attract because each half can offer what the other lacks and needs.

Misunderstandings can also arise through lack of communication, and a casual talk in informal surroundings can often restore confidence. A common basis can be found, and an apparent enemy can turn into a friend. Even people who seem ugly or hostile at first can then reveal their friendly sides.

'Birds of a feather flock together because they share a common background. And opposites attract because each half can offer what the other lacks and needs.'

離兌
上下
睽小事吉彖曰睽火動而上澤動而下二

Changing Lines

Bottom Line   If he argues with people who are really his own kind, they will eventually find back to him. But if he has to deal with people who are not his kind, there will never be a real friendship.

Second Line   When he disagrees with people who are important to him, a casually arranged and confidential chat will usually help to clear the air.

Third Line   If he feels opposed or disgraced in public, he need not always take this personally. Perhaps he only got into the way of strange people or circumstances, and the incident will soon be forgotten.

Fourth Line   In the face of general opposition he may feel isolated at first. But soon he discovers that there are others who share his ideas.

Fifth Line   When he finds people who share his background or who experience life as he does, a natural harmony results.

Top Line   Sometimes he will meet strangers who seem ugly and evil at first. He gets ready to attack them but then finds to his surprise that they are decent people underneath.

39. Dealing with Difficulties

When one, seeing the peril, can arrest his steps, is he not wise?
... The superior man, in accordance with this, turns round and
examines himself, and cultivates his virtue.

We can deal with obstacles along the path in various ways. The sooner we see them, the better we can handle them, and through flexible manoeuvres we may be able to avoid most of them altogether.

The stone that is a stumbling block to one person may serve as a comfortable seat for another person. People who keep complaining about the rough road when others enjoy a smooth journey with occasional challenges, need to examine their attitude toward life. Most likely they tend to blame their circumstances and other people for their own mistakes. By condemning others they gain a sense of superiority and avoid the effort of self-adjustment.

Good timing may also help to avoid an obstruction: what is very difficult and problematic today may take care of itself tomorrow – or vice versa. And sometimes it is best to stay on familiar ground, instead of venturing out into risky areas. The potential rewards of an expedition may not be worth the problems and frustration that are bound to emerge along the way.

At home we know what we have, we can enjoy the company of friends and neighbours. In any case we can often achieve more at home than abroad. Here we have access to many people and tools which we would miss along the way. We also save energy by staying in one place.

But life evolves, and eventually we have to go out and explore new avenues. Inevitably there will be some obstacles along the way. To overcome the more serious ones we will need the help of reliable allies and/or the advice of experienced persons. But above all we have to be confident of our own inner strength.

坎艮
上下
蹇利西南不利東北以西
南之地也東北山也
難之平則難解以也

'When one, seeing the peril, can arrest his steps, is he not wise?'

Changing Lines

Bottom Line When he notices friction, he hesitates and examines his course. He clarifies the issue and waits for the right moment before he continues.

Second Line If he has no control over the problem, and no doubts about his approach, the only thing he can do is struggle on and hope for the best.

Third Line Instead of venturing out into risky areas, he returns to familiar ground and enjoys the company of his own people.

Fourth Line Are the hoped-for rewards worth the trouble and frustrations? Or should he go home and enjoy the little things that count?

Fifth Line When difficulties mount, he will need to mobilize his inner strength. He may also need the help of reliable friends and the advice of experienced people.

Top Line There are times when he can achieve more by staying where he is than by moving forward. An experienced ally or his own conscience can tell him how to make the best of what he already has.

坎上艮下

蹇利西南不利東北以西南地也東北山也

難之平則難解以

40.   Clearing the Air

If some operations be called for, there will be good fortune in the early conducting of them. ... The superior man, in accordance with this, forgives errors and deals gently with crimes.

After days of oppressive heat, a thunderstorm clears the air and sets the stage for new growth in the fields. When people have been living under tense circumstances, a swift decision can often untie knotted nerves and restore the inner and outer balance. But this must be done smoothly and efficiently. The purpose is not to correct or to punish, but to release tension and to restore normal conditions.

Under nerve-wracking circumstances we may feel tempted to project our tense ideas and to impose new rules or structures on things and people, which would only add to the tension. If instead we calmly isolate the problem and untie the knot that lies at its root, things can automatically revert to their natural state. There is then no need to set drastic examples or to punish offenders, because the root of the problem has been removed and potential conflicts have been defused.

But a certain frankness and directness is called for when a sly habit or a devious person has to be dealt with. In such cases it is best to come straight to the point and to call things by their real names, so that no doubts remain.

Tension can also be the result of an overly ambitious and pretentious way of life. By showing off we provoke envy and criticism, and by displaying our power or possessions we invite opposition and robbery. But as soon as we abandon such artificial habits we can enjoy life once more and find our inner peace.

'After days of oppressive heat, a thunderstorm clears the air and sets the stage for new growth in the fields.'

Changing Lines

Bottom Line　If he proceeds with an innocent desire to restore the natural balance, everything will fall into place.

Second Line　If tension has been created by cunning schemes or foxy people, he comes straight to the point and unties the knot at the root of the problem.

Third Line　Instead of leading a pretentious life to impress others, he relaxes and finds himself. By doing so he also avoids arousing envy and the possibility of robbery.

Fourth Line　As soon as he abandons petty or low desires, he will find true friends who understand him.

Fifth Line　By setting things straight and clearing away improper elements, he can gain his inner balance and the confidence of others.

Top Line　If he can defuse an irritating problem or neutralize an aggressive trouble maker, conditions will return to normal.

震坎
上下
解利西南也亦往不困于東北故不言不利衆

西南衆也解難濟險利施於衆

41. Decrease and Increase

There is a time when the strong should be diminished and the weak should be strengthened. Diminution and increase, overflowing and emptiness: these take place in harmony with conditions of the time.

There is a constant exchange of energy between people, between high and low, between the individual and the community. A surplus in one place soon finds its way to another place where it is needed. Wealthy individuals give to the poor or pay their share to the community and, in turn, the communal wealth is spread to benefit all.

But such an exchange should not lead to a levelling of all differences. The generous benefactor should ask himself if the poor and downtrodden really deserve his help and if they are doing all they can to help themselves. Too much charity depletes the general affluence and demoralizes the recipients. Excessive taxes weaken the initiative of ambitious individuals and justify the laziness of those who like to depend on free handouts.

A certain amount of self-discipline and self-criticism is needed to strengthen individual self-reliance and to eliminate poverty. Help is gladly given to the person who is sincerely trying to help himself and/or to correct his shortcomings. Even heaven seems to help those who help themselves. This, in turn, enables such people later to share their good fortune with those who are truly in need through no fault of their own.

兌上損有孚元吉无咎可貞利有攸往曷之用

'There is a constant exchange of energy between people, between high and low, between the individual and the community.'

Changing Lines

Bottom Line He wants to share his wealth and good fortune with others and hurries to help them. If his intentions are sincere, much good will come from this. But will he go overboard in his generosity? Is someone giving or accepting too much?

Second Line In his eagerness to be generous he may throw himself away. He may volunteer to support those who do not really deserve help.

Third Line The person who walks alone soon finds a partner. Together they can form a natural union. But if a third one joins them, discord and jealousy arise, and one of them has to leave.

Fourth Line If he manages to reduce his problems and shortcomings, others will feel more at ease with him and more inclined to help him. Even if his circumstances are unfavourable, his sincere desire for improvement and self-improvement will be noticed.

Fifth Line Everything will be added to the deserving person who lives in harmony with himself and the cosmic forces. There is no need to act in a selfish manner because higher forces work in his favour.

Top Line He shares in the abundance of creation and enriches the lives of others, without decreasing his own wealth. By thus acting in the right spirit, everything he does will be of mutual and general benefit.

兌上·損有孚元吉无咎可貞利有攸往曷之用

42. The Harvest

巽上震下．益。利有攸往。利涉大川象曰益損上益下。

The superior man, in accordance with this, when he sees what is good, moves towards it; and when he sees his errors, he turns from them.

The Yi hexagram shows how to make good use of opportunities. When the harvest is ripe, no time should be wasted in bringing it in. When a favourable situation presents itself, bold action is called for to take advantage of it, even if this may involve some risk.

But such action should spring from a sincere heart, not from greed and selfishness. Those who try to increase their fortune at other people's expense or with ulterior motives will not be able to enjoy their apparent gains in the end. And those who pretend to help others but are really motivated by selfish aims will encounter resentment and even attacks from unexpected quarters.

This is why any increase in the outer world brings more satisfaction if it is preceded by an increase of inner purity. The person who harmonizes with the cosmic forces and acts with a sincere desire to support a worthwhile cause will increase his fortune in one way or another, even under unfavourable conditions, when others are suffering. Because he acts from his centre and is not swayed by superficial appearances, he can often act as a guide to those who feel confused deep down. He has access to the abundance of creation and generously shares his inner riches with others.

'When the harvest is ripe, no time should be wasted in bringing it in.'

Changing Lines

Bottom Line When opportunities offer themselves, he takes advantage of them, although this may seem to involve some risk. The beneficial results will justify his boldness in the end.

Second Line As soon as the time is ripe and the indications are favourable, he begins with the harvest. He works for a worthwhile cause and is not motivated by greed or selfish aims. His efforts are rewarded with success.

Third Line He turns seemingly unfavourable conditions to his favour, while others are struggling with difficulties. By persevering modestly and sincerely, he gains benefits for himself and others.

Fourth Line Through his sincere attitude and experience he can often advise others and give a new direction to the common cause, so that all are going to benefit.

Fifth Line He is in a position to help others, and he acts with kindness. All those involved acknowledge his sincerity and benefit from his generosity. ,

Top Line If his intentions are not really sincere when he pretends to help others, this will cause resentment and even invite attacks by outsiders. Therefore he first purifies his heart, so that he can act without selfishness.

43. Determination

He must openly denounce the criminal and seek to awaken general sympathy, and at the same time go about his enterprise, conscious of its difficulty and danger. ... He must make it understood how unwillingly he takes up arms.

The person who struggles on alone must be alert and prepared for unforeseen difficulties. If others find him/her too aggressive, they might put additional obstacles in his way. Therefore he will want to keep his eyes and ears open to sense approaching trouble. He will find it wise to follow a reasonable middle path that does not arouse hostility.

The person who moves on alone also needs to be strongly motivated and firmly convinced of his/her goal if he wants to succeed. Vague desires and half-hearted attempts are not enough to turn things in his favour. His efforts would also be undermined by needless worry and lacking faith.

Whenever you are faced with difficulties along your path in life, you will be tempted to become a fanatical loner with hate in your heart. If this becomes a habit, you will end up hating yourself, as well as most of the people around you and the world in general. Your associates will then sense your cynical attitude and avoid you. Soon you will be left with the dubious company of those who share your negative views.

But if instead you follow the sane middle path and cultivate worthwhile social relationships, your doubts and worries will disappear. You will know that you can rely on the goodwill of others and on the support of nature. By being in tune with your own centre you will attract the right people and circumstances.

兌上。乾下。夬揚于王庭孚號有厲告自邑不利即戎。

'The person who struggles on alone must be alert and prepared for difficulties.'

Changing Lines

Bottom Line If he is motivated only by petty desires and fails to put his whole weight behind his project, he will not succeed.

Second Line As long as he is alert and prepared for unforeseen difficulties, he need not worry about the future. Help will come if the need should arise.

Third Line If he struggles on with too much determination, and with hate in his heart, he will in the end be disliked by his own friends.

Fourth Line If he is unwilling to learn from life or to listen to his own heart, his progress will be slow and full of obstacles.

Fifth Line When he pulls up weeds and undesirable elements, does he act from his centre and avoid extremes? Or is he guided by destructive urges and a desire for vengeance?

Top Line Instead of struggling on like a lonely fanatic, he takes time out to cultivate friendships and to become aware of other people's problems.

兌下。
夬揚于王庭孚號有厲告自邑不利即戎。

44. Encroachment

乾巽
上下
姤。
女壯。
勿用取女。象曰姤。遇也。柔遇剛也。

Kau shows a female who is bold and strong. It will not be good to marry such a female.

There are times when the Yang (male) forces retreat and the Yin (female) forces move forward. In the evening, for example, the light fades and darkness takes over. During long periods of peace the men tend to become softer and the women stronger. These changes of emphasis are part of life, they are basically neither good nor bad. But they can become undesirable when the balance is lost and the Yin element begins to dominate. This is the case when an aggressive woman manipulates a man, or when a permissive man lets such a woman dominate him. On the individual level the same conditions arise when someone loses control of his life and is dominated by unreasonable and unpredictable emotions.

Yin and Yang need each other, and neither should try to repress or dominate the other. Whenever the heart (Yin) encroaches on the domain of the head (Yang), the result is chaos and decadence. If, on the other hand, the head begins to repress the heart, an equally undesirable condition arises which results in mental rigidity and arrogance. In the context of society this means that people in leading positions should be reasonable and understanding, but that they should not let their followers dominate them.

Similarly you will want to maintain a subtle balance between your thoughts and your feelings in your daily life, between your desire to dominate and your desire to understand and flow with the tide. You can listen to your heart and yet remain the master of your fate.

'You can listen to your heart and yet remain the master of your fate.'

Changing Lines

Bottom Line If he is guided by unreasonable and unpredictable feelings, he will lose control of his life and jump around like a wild pig.

Second Line Instead of letting emotions or servants dominate him, he remains master of the situation and does not open his heart to everybody.

Third Line By staying mentally detached he avoids emotional involvement with unworthy ideas and people. He does not let circumstances dominate him.

Fourth Line If he ignores his heart and represses his emotions, he will soon be alienated from his inner self and from other people.

Fifth Line He can be master of the situation without imposing his will on others or displaying his brilliance. By cultivating a subtle and considerate attitude he can enjoy the goodwill of others and the support of nature.

Top Line Does he look down upon the world and react defensively or aggressively when people approach him? Such an attitude would bring humiliation.

乾巽
上下
姤。
女壯。
勿用取女。
象曰姤。
遇也。
柔遇剛也。

45. The Happy Union

It will be advantageous to meet the great man, and there will then be prosperity and success. The union effected by him will be on and through what is correct.

A person's success or failure in life is to a great extent determined by the people with whom he associates, and by the kind of relationhips he/she cultivates with them. More serious and lasting bonds should therefore be entered into with open eyes. A certain amount of gravity and ceremony is called for, together with a deep awareness of the consequences and responsibilities involved. The advice of an experienced man or woman can often make the difference.

When a solitary person appears happy on the surface, others will tend to assume that he/she has no real need for intimate relationships. But very often such a person feels sad and lonely underneath. By talking openly about this, the pretence is abandoned and a union with like-minded people becomes possible.

The best friendships emerge spontaneously, from the heart, they cannot be created by conscious effort. When a union becomes forced and artificial, it is best to abandon it gracefully.

To find like-minded people is not always easy, and one should not try to associate intimately with everybody and anybody. But on the other hand it would be unrealistic to look for perfection in people. Those who set their standards too high will lead cold and solitary lives.

Occasional solitude is beneficial, because it makes the union with the 'inner self' possible and leads to inner harmony. In the end we all have the friends we deserve. By becoming better persons we can enjoy better relationships with more worthwhile people.

'A person's success or failure in life is to a great extent determined by the people with whom he/she associates.'

Changing Lines

Bottom Line He would like to join others, but remains alone at first. When he makes his desires clear, he finds a happy union with like-minded people, and all is well.

Second Line Like-minded people are drawn to each other spontaneously, without conscious effort. When they sincerely appreciate each other and show this through tokens of friendship, a happy union results.

Third Line He feels lonely and sad because he does not meet compatible people, until he realizes that his standards are too demanding. A more realistic attitude reveals many worthwhile people around him.

Fourth Line When he associates with others, he asks himself if they are his kind of people. Should this be a casual or a more intimate union?

Fifth Line His beneficial influence encourages harmonious relationships between all concerned, and everybody feels appreciated. If some of them do not trust him at first, he assures them of his sincerity and his long-term commitment.

Top Line When others misunderstand or abandon him, he sighs and weeps at first. But then he realizes that his isolation is not his fault, and he feels good again.

兌坤
上下。
萃亨。
（萃聚
）乃
在通
季也
反。
○
王
假
有
廟。
聚假
至至
有也王
廟以
也。

46.   Building up Slowly

The superior man, in accordance with this, pays careful attention to his virtue, and accumulates the small developments of it until it is high and great.

During the growing season, plants and trees follow the trend of the time and push upward. They grow step by step, gradually and patiently, until they are fully grown.

In the same way people can observe how their projects develop gradually, and how they realize their goals by patiently adding one element after another, just as a home is built brick by brick. They can attain the position they deserve by performing a useful service and by slowly accumulating credit. But those who hurry through life restlessly and impatiently will find that they are often overtaken by others who did not attempt to skip any stages of development.

This is not the time to force the way up or to push ahead against the tide. But whenever circumstances are especially favourable, it may be wise to move ahead swiftly and to make use of certain opportunities that offer themselves.

While things are progressing at their natural pace, it is important to keep a sense of proportion and not to get carried away. If success is allowed to become an end in itself, it loses its meaning and leads to disaster. Progress is desirable only as long as it serves a worthwhile goal. This is why people can remain truly successful only as long as they keep in touch with their own conscience, with wise counsel and with the cosmic order.

'During the growing season, plants and trees follow the trend of the time and push upward. They grow step by step, gradually and patiently.'

Changing Lines

Bottom Line   The time is favourable for moving up slowly. As long as he is guided by divine inspiration, he will enjoy the support of the right people.

Second Line   Although he may not have much to offer, he performs his function with sincerity and loyalty, and receives his reward.

Third Line   When things are going well, he will want to push ahead boldly and take advantage of unusual opportunities. But he needs to make sure that his success does not lead him into careless impatience and opportunism.

Fourth Line   While he is moving up the ladder of success, he listens to his conscience that tells him what is right. He keeps in touch with the right people and with the cosmic powers that give his progress direction and meaning.

Fifth Line   He takes the steps up the ladder of success one at a time, not skipping important stages. To jump erratically and hastily would invite accidents and retard his progress.

Top Line   Each upward move requires careful attention. Those who push up blindly and greedily will soon get into trouble. If success becomes an end in itself, it leads to failure. But if it promotes a worthy cause, all involved will benefit.

坤上
巽下

升元亨。
用見大人。
勿恤。

巽順
可以升陽爻
不當尊位以无升
嚴剛

47. Adversity

Who is it but the superior man that, though straightened, still does not fail in making progress to his proper end?

A tree may at times encounter resistance in its growth, when it is unable to spread its branches or roots, or when it lacks water during dry periods. Similarly, you may now and then feel constrained in your efforts and projects, you may feel exhausted or you may fall into a state of gloom and depression. During such times it may seem to you that everything you do is in vain and that whatever you try to tell others is misunderstood or rejected.

To go on under such circumstances requires much faith, strong principles and a willingness to correct yourself whenever you have lost the right path. It is, for instance, entirely possible that you have brought on part of the gloom yourself, and that you can therefore remove part of the obstacles yourself by adopting a more realistic attitude. If you are strong and honest enough to do this, you may turn a seeming defeat into victory, and you may find that there is plenty of room to grow if you grow in the right direction and if you regain your vision.

The mark of a great person is his/her ability to turn failure into success, to go on cheerfully in the face of resistance. Those who lack the necessary inner resources, resilience and conviction soon fall by the wayside during lean periods.

But even in times of apparent prosperity you will sometimes feel tied down by a multitude of little strings and frustrations. You then need to regain your mental focus, by temporarily withdrawing from the outer confusion and rediscovering the vision that gives direction and meaning to your life.

'A tree may at times encounter resistance in its growth, when it is unable to spread its branches or roots, or when it lacks water during dry periods.'

Changing Lines

Bottom Line If he loses his vision and true goal in life, there will be no end to the obstacles in his path. He will feel constrained, tied down, chained by circumstances. He will stumble along like a slave, not free to do what he really wants.

Second Line When he is pestered by many little frustrations, and most of what he does seems to go wrong, it is time to seek wise counsel or guidance.

Third Line Sometimes he is confused and overlooks important facts and clues, he ignores people and stumbles into thorny situations. In such cases he needs to sit down, drop his preconceived ideas, find his own centre and set new goals.

Fourth Line If he perseveres patiently in a worthy cause, the right actions will accumulate and everything will turn out well. Otherwise his progress will be slow and cumbersome.

Fifth Line By maintaining a humble and sincere attitude, he turns things to his favour. He can move again. As soon as he regains his self-confidence, others will have more confidence in him.

Top Line Is he going in the wrong direction? He hesitates to make a move because he is tied down by many little frustrations. But if he corrects himself, things will start moving again and he will reach his goal.

兌下
坎上

困亨。

窮必通也。處窮而不失其亨

能自通者小人也

貞大人吉无咎

坎巽
上下

井。
改邑不改井。
井□以不□
變爲德
領反者
无喪无

48. The Deep Well

A well supplies nourishment and is not itself exhausted. The superior man, in accordance with this, comforts the people and stimulates them to mutual helpfulness.

In ancient times, settlements were built around the well. Village life revolved around the source of water. Although a supply of food was also necessary, water was even more basic and essential. Thus, the deep well is often taken as a symbol of basic life energy that is shared by all and without which human beings cannot exist. Governments and generations come and go, but this basic source of vitality remains.

However, wells have to be taken care of and they have to be kept clean. Leaks must be repaired so that the water is not wasted. In the same way communities and individuals must cultivate their source of inner strength. They must avoid wasting their precious life energy on inferior or frivolous pursuits. They need to set aside time to cultivate their contact with the cosmic powers, through daily meditation and periodic ceremonies.

We can experience the very source of this life force when we are silent and in touch with the inner self. In such quiet moments we suddenly become aware of the truth that was there in front of us all the time. Our creative energies are awakened and we know at once how to deal with everyday situations that seemed so perplexing before. Such ingenuity and creativity is not the privilege of a few but the birthright of all. Everybody can make use of the 'deep well' within.

'A deep well is often taken as a symbol of basic life energy that is shared by all and without which human beings cannot exist.'

坎巽
上下
井改
邑不
改井。

𠊳
（井）
精
領
反。

以
不
變
為
德
者

无
喪
无

Changing Lines

Bottom Line   He will succeed if he keeps the source of his vitality pure. People who neglect their inner strength resemble those who are satisfied with water from a muddy well.

Second Line   If he dissipates his vital energies, he is like one who depends on a well that leaks and leaves the water to fish and slugs.

Third Line   A good well is useless if nobody drinks from it. Is he making good use of his potential and his source of life energy?

Fourth Line   Just as a well has to be kept in good repair, people need to cultivate their source of vitality. Therefore he sets aside part of his time for this purpose.

Fifth Line   At the very bottom of the well is the point from which pure and refreshing water wells up. Deep within himself he can find the source of pure life energy.

Top Line   The well is located in the centre of the village, and the water is there for all to use. Everybody has access to the cosmic life energy.

49. Profound Changes

*The change is viewed by people generally with suspicion and
dislike, and should not be made hastily. When made as a
necessity, and its good effects are obvious, the result will be
great and good.*

Certain animals, like birds and snakes, change their
feathers and skins periodically. Even the human body is
practically rebuilt about once a year: the billions of living
cells that form it are continuously dying and being
replaced by new ones.

Although change is part of life, it should not be seen as
an end in itself.

Stability is also essential for survival. A thing or idea
needs to be replaced only after it has outlived its
usefulness. To alter established rules or habits requires
much effort, and the end result may not justify the
inconvenience. This is why the I Ching warns against
hasty and premature innovations. Novel ideas often
promise more than they can actually fulfil, they tend to
upset old – and perhaps valuable – habits and belief
systems, and they can strain relationships between
people.

But when a change does become necessary, it needs to
be contemplated thoroughly and repeatedly before action
is taken. All those who will be involved must be
consulted, and all aspects must be openly discussed until
everybody is satisfied and fully convinced. Any
remaining questions should be answered and all doubts
removed.

Especially the leader or initiator ought to be fully
convinced and able to convince others. Otherwise people
may just agree superficially and later continue in their old
ways. But when the ground is well prepared and the plans
well thought out, the new order will easily take root and
create a new harmony.

'His change of direction should be sincere and obvious to all, and marked in clear lines like the stripes of a tiger.'

Changing Lines

Bottom Line If he is tied to senseless habits or traditions, and his attitude is hidebound, he will benefit from gradual changes.

Second Line After he has thoroughly thought about the issue and waited for the right time, he can successfully introduce changes step by step.

Third Line When he has repeatedly thought about the needed change, and discussed it three times with all involved, everybody will be ready. Is there anything else that should be taken into consideration?

Fourth Line When changing established rules or deep-seated habits, he needs to be fully convinced and able to convince others through his enthusiasm.

Fifth Line His change of direction should be sincere and obvious to all, and marked in clear lines like the stripes of a tiger.

Top Line When a change is needed, he completes it thoroughly to the last detail. He does not merely change his face and smile obediently, while secretly acting in the old way.

離下
兌上
革。

巳日乃孚元亨利貞悔亡。

夫民可與習常，難與適變。

50.　Proper Means and Ends

三三

離巽
上下
鼎。
元
吉
亨。

The sages cooked their offerings in order to present them to the gods, and made great feasts to nourish their wise and able ministers.

Before a ceremonial meal is prepared, all pots and utensils must be thoroughly cleaned. Before people set out on important projects, they need to purify their minds and establish the proper habits and arrangements. If a tool or possession does not fit this pattern, it may have to be reshaped. If a person is not up to the job, he/she may have to be educated or trained.

Thus, when you have pure intentions and a worthwhile goal, and use the means that do justice to the ends, the details of your projects will take care of themselves. Your achievements will be great and they will be noticed. Some small-minded people may envy you, but they cannot harm you because your intentions are unselfish.

But if you use inferior means or rely on the wrong type of people, your projects will fail because they lack the necessary support. The same would happen if you made ambitious plans but lacked the experience or capability to carry them out. And if you were experienced and capable, but pursued an unworthy goal, you would be equally unsuccessful.

But even if you have the best intentions and use the proper approach, you will at times encounter obstacles on your path. This is when you will need patience and perseverance to carry on until the harvest is ripe and you can enjoy the fruits of your efforts.

人革去故而法制齊明吉然後乃其

易故而鼎取新取新而當其

'Before a ceremonial meal is prepared, all pots and utensils must be thoroughly cleaned.'

Changing Lines

Bottom Line Before cooking he cleans the pots. Before embarking on a new venture he clears his mind of obsolete and preconceived ideas.

Second Line When he achieves something in the pursuit of a worthy cause, small-minded people may envy him. But they cannot harm him because his intentions are pure.

Third Line Even though he may have the purest intentions, his progress will at times be obstructed. But if he proceeds with patience and moderation, the tension will dissolve in the end.

Fourth Line If he has built on weak foundations, used inferior means or relied on the wrong people, his project will collapse and he will lose the fruits of his efforts.

Fifth Line By using a moderate approach and by pursuing a worthwhile goal, all the details in his life fall into place and he moves on.

Top Line If his efforts are dedicated to a worthy goal and his intentions are sincere, anything he undertakes in this spirit will be beneficial.

離巽
上下

鼎。

元吉亨。

人革易故故而而法鼎制取齊新明取吉新然而後當乃其

51. Times of Turmoil

When the time of movement comes, he will be found looking out with apprehension and yet smiling and talking cheerfully. The result is that he adopts proper laws for his course.

People may dread a thunderstorm, but in a way we also look forward to it with excited expectation, because we know that it will release built-up tension and bring the rain that is needed by the earth. Such storms may sometimes cause floods or start fires through lightning, but in the end things come back to normal and everybody feels relieved.

In times of turmoil our attitude can make the difference between success and failure. Although we should take the necessary precautions and look ahead with some concern, there is no need to panic or to fret and worry. In the coming upheaval we may lose some of our privileges or possessions, but we may also encounter unexpected opportunities, and in the end we may even gain. In any case we can be confident that the lost things we really need and deserve will eventually come back to us. Certain possessions are really burdens anyway, and to lose them would be a blessing.

For manoeuvring in chaotic circumstances we need an alert and flexible attitude. If we lose our mental clarity or cling to preconceived ideas, each new change will add to our confusion and get us deeper into the mire. But a calm and adaptable mind can easily handle the shocks that would cause most people to panic. Although such a state of mind may seem indifferent or blasé to others, it allows us to save our energies and to reach our goal unharmed.

震下震上。震。亨。震來虩虩。笑言啞啞。震之義。

'A calm and adaptable mind can easily handle the shocks that would cause most people to panic.'

Changing Lines

Bottom Line   When great changes are in the making, he does not panic. He remains calm because he knows that the tension will be released after the storm, and that things will find a new balance.

Second Line   In times of upheaval he will be in danger and he may lose some of his privileges and possessions. But the things he really needs and deserves will eventually come back to him.

Third Line   When the turmoil around him threatens to upset him, he can prevent confusion and accidents through mental detachment. He should not undertake anything while in a nervous state of mind.

Fourth Line   If he loses his mental clarity and procrastinates, he will sink deeper into the mud with each change.

Fifth Line   Startling changes bring peril and possible loss, but also opportunities and the chance of gain.

Top Line   If the turmoil causes him to panic and to lose his inner balance, everything he does will be unlucky. But he can remain calm even when others panic, although they may then call him indifferent.

震上震下。震亨。是以懼以成。則震來虩虩。笑言啞啞。震之爲義。

52. Keeping Calm

Ken denotes resting when it is time to rest, and acting when it is time to act. The superior man, in accordance with this, does not go in his thoughts beyond the position in which he is.

This hexagram is symbolized by the mountain, the immovable and unshakeable centre, surrounded by valleys, rivers, fields and forests. On the human level, Ken represents the spine, the central axis of the body and nervous system. All limbs hinge on the spine, the head balances on top, and the nerves that connect all parts of the body extend inside it.

By keeping the spine still we can calm the entire nervous system together with the mind and the heart. If before we have been plagued by doubts, frustrations and feelings of guilt, we suddenly sense a refreshing and rejuvenating inner peace. Anxious and ego-centred thoughts disappear. Where before we felt uncertain and insecure, we now experience a blissful certainty. We are in tune with our inner self and in harmony with the cosmic order.

With some practice you can maintain this state of inner calm also in your everyday life, while engaged in activities and while interacting with others. Your thoughts and actions will then become more balanced and effective. Your speech will be more sensible and convincing. Your relationships become less ego-centred and more stable. Your body movements originate in your gravity centre around the hips and not nervously from the shoulders or limbs.

When you are centred in this way, others will sense it. They will wonder what your secret is and how they can learn it. But you can teach them more by your example than through words.

'This hexagram is symbolized by the mountain, the immovable and unshakeable centre, surrounded by valleys, rivers, fields and forests.'

Changing Lines

Bottom Line If he keeps calm at the subtle beginning stage, he can build on a solid foundation, like someone who keeps his toes still.

Second Line When things are already underway, he makes sure that he walks along calmly, in a continuous movement. If others push ahead nervously, he can rarely help them.

Third Line His gravity centre around the hips is by nature quiet. Movements and feelings originate from it. By calming it further he would stifle his heart.

Fourth Line By keeping his trunk and spine still, he calms his arms and legs and his head. Thus he avoids needless agitation, confusion, doubts and frustration.

Fifth Line He keeps his jaws at rest and avoids nervous and senseless talk. When his speech is calm and sincere, others will listen and be convinced.

Top Line By remaining calm and centred deep down, all he thinks and does will be beneficial.

艮上
艮下

艮其背（艮目）根恨（艮也）。

不獲其身

無患也

故所止在其後。

53. Gradual Advance

The advance indicated by Chien is like the marrying of a young lady. ... In restfulness and flexible penetration we have a movement that is inexhaustible.

A lasting relationship like marriage does not develop overnight. It takes shape gradually and requires a certain amount of ceremony. In this hexagram it is symbolized by the pairing of geese, who are said to unite for life. The process of courtship develops in a sequence of stages, each having a distinct function and leading up to marriage.

The first stage is characterized by uncertainty and doubts. You have found a partner or position that seems promising, but you are not yet sure of yourself and you are afraid of criticism. You are putting out feelers to see how people will react. You feel like a bird of passage that has finally reached a safe but unknown shore.

Gradually you find your bearings and you become familiar with the circumstances and people. You begin to feel appreciated and you find that you can do something useful for others. Consequently your needs are taken care of, you can enjoy food and drink and be happy in the company of compatible people.

This affluence and ease will tend to make you over-confident, however. You may now feel that everything you do will turn out in your favour, and that failure is out of the question. Thus you will be tempted to strike out on risky adventures in unknown territory. Soon your resources will be exhausted, the people who depend on you will suffer, and you may fall into inferior company.

Affluence may also tempt you to become overly ambitious and to rise into the clouds above. Up there you will feel somewhat lonely and cold. But your efforts and achievements can serve to enhance the culture that benefits all people.

'A lasting relationship ... is symbolized by the pairing of geese, who are said to unite for life.'

Changing Lines

Bottom Line   After he has finally found a resting place, he still has to get settled. Some uncertainties remain; he still has doubts and feels exposed to criticism.

Second Line   When he finds a solid foundation and earns a comfortable living, he can enjoy food and drink and share his good fortune.

Third Line   If he sets out on risky ventures with high ambitions, his reserves will dwindle, his dependants will suffer, and he may fall among bad company.

Fourth Line   Highly elevated places may seem desirable. But he will find them uncomfortable and unsuitable. To keep from falling down he will have to look for a reasonably safe place.

Fifth Line   When he reaches the summit, he discovers that life up there is somewhat cold and sterile. It takes him some time to regain his vitality and productivity.

Top Line   If he chooses to live in the clouds and dedicate his life to high ideals, his achievements will add to the culture that benefits all people.

艮下
巽上
漸。
女歸吉利貞。

以漸者漸進之卦也。止而巽。
斯漸適進。
進漸者也。止以止

54. Being Useful

震兑
上下
歸
妹。
征
凶
无
攸
利。

嫁者少女之稱也兑爲少陰而爲

妹者少陰震爲長陽

The marriage of a younger sister is the end of her maidenhood and the beginning of her motherhood. ... The superior man, in accordance with this, having regard to the far-distant end, knows the mischief that may be done at the beginning.

Finding a suitable relationship or place in life is not always easy. This hexagram illustrates the difficulties and shows how to overcome them, through the example of a younger sister, a girl who has little to offer in the way of a dowry or other qualities. The text shows that even people who are limping on one leg or who are blind in one eye can find their place in life and fulfil a useful function, as long as they adapt to the situation and do not cling to exaggerated expectations.

Similarly, you will sometimes find yourself in a situation where a suitable partner or position is not available, or where your better qualities are not appreciated. You have then the choice of either waiting for things to improve, or of accepting the available position until a better one comes along. If the position is really below your dignity, you may not want to bother with it. But if you do accept it, you should be prepared to play the part and to fulfil the requirements without moaning or displaying your superiority.

When you become involved in a group or community, you will probably be expected to participate in the games, ceremonies or parties, and to contribute to them. It would then be embarrassing to arrive at such occasions with empty hands or unwilling to participate. The right thing to do would be to become part of the scene and to offer your assistance.

'The marriage of a younger sister is the end of her maidenhood and the beginning of her motherhood.'

Changing Lines

Bottom Line Even a person who is lame in one leg can find happiness. If he knows what he has to offer and is aware of his shortcomings, he can be certain that a suitable position or relationship will come along sooner or later.

Second Line Someone who does not see well can use his other talents to make himself useful. But he should be realistic and maintain his reserve and modesty.

Third Line If he cannot find a suitable partner or position, he may have to accept a compromise for the time being, and make the best of it. By resenting the situation he would only hurt himself.

Fourth Line If the available positions are below his dignity and would involve him with inferior company, he prefers not to throw himself away. Instead, he waits until the situation changes.

Fifth Line When he enters into a relationship with a handicap, or when some of his qualities are not appreciated, he adapts to the situation and reduces his expectations.

Top Line If he has nothing to contribute to the communal project or ceremony, he cannot really become part of the group, and people will not fully accept him.

55. The Time to Prosper

Let him be as the sun at noon: it is for him to cause his light to shine on all under the sky.

The Feng hexagram describes the conditions under which people can become more prosperous and enlightened. Just as plants grow in certain seasons and not in others, there are certain times when prosperity is more easily attained. But even during leaner periods one can assure a degree of affluence by following the principles laid out here.

For example, people need to have something in common, and they need to share a common goal to increase their prosperity. As long as they misunderstand and work against each other, their achievements will be limited.

But even then, some people may have closed minds, they may not be able to see the obvious road to riches. Lecturing would make them only more stubborn in their mistaken beliefs. They can only be convinced through the example of someone actually attaining the success they crave deep down.

As soon as the truth becomes obvious, even the most rigid and sluggish minds begin to pay attention and to take action. The more intelligent people can now form a team and set up the conditions that will bring prosperity to all. The necessities of all involved will then be taken care of, and the higher needs can find their fulfilment.

But because leaner times will come sooner or later, some miserly people will be tempted to hoard their riches and to close their doors to friends and family. They will then suffer from their self-imposed isolation. It will take them some time to understand that true prosperity is created and maintained by the process of exchanging things, thoughts and feelings for mutual benefit.

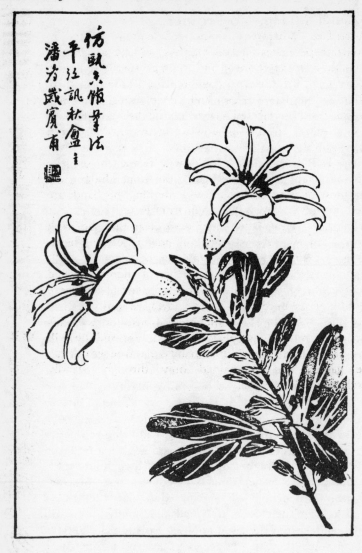

'Just as plants grow in certain seasons and not in others, there are certain times when prosperity is more easily attained.'

Changing Lines

Bottom Line When two or more people are motivated by similar experiences and convictions, and by a common goal, they can move ahead and attain prosperity together.

Second Line If he tries to enlighten the less informed by pointing out the obvious and by lecturing them, his message will be rejected and he will be disliked. But if he sets a sincere example of how to do things, people will follow him.

Third Line Sometimes people will refuse to see the obvious facts, and nobody will join him. Under such circumstances he is unable to do anything, his hands are tied. But his sincerity saves him from error.

Fourth Line If the facts become so clear that the truth finally dawns on the most rigid minds, people will begin to listen to him, and joint action can be taken.

Fifth Line By gathering more intelligent and enlightened people around him, he attains prosperity for all, and there will be occasion for praise and congratulations.

Top Line If he closes the door to his house and keeps his riches to himself, people will avoid him and he will become isolated. He will then realize that true wealth can be gained and maintained only through friendly exchanges with people.

離下
震上
豐亨王假之（假
庚白反又古雅反○
勿憂

大而亨者王之所至
者王之所至

56. The Traveller

There may be some small attainment and progress. If the stranger or traveller be firm and correct as he ought to be, there will be good fortune.

On our path through life we pass through many stages and situations, and thus we often experience the joys and sorrows of the proverbial traveller or stranger. Like birds of passage we build our nests here and there, always aware of the possibility that they may be burgled, burned down or otherwise lost. We take care of our possessions as well as we can, we try to live on good terms with our associates and neighbours, and we manage to make a living. But soon the conditions may change and we may have to move on.

In your role as a wanderer through life you are exposed to the dangers of the road. You may get involved with inferior people or with projects that are below your dignity. You are at the mercy of the people whom you meet on the way. This is why you need to be careful, alert, flexible and polite. As a stranger you are subject to the laws of the host country and you have fewer rights than the people who belong there. Even if you feel that you have been cheated or hurt by a local person, you would be foolish to denounce your opponent publicly and to assert yourself noisily.

It is better to win the trust and friendship of your neighbours first. Especially if you hope to advance to a more favourable position, you need to cultivate the goodwill of influential people. By carefully preparing the ground you can create a safe and comfortable environment in which you feel at home.

'In your role as a wanderer through life you are exposed to the dangers of the road.'

Changing Lines

Bottom Line While he is underway, he may come in contact with dubious people and get involved with trivial projects. Thus he remains polite but reserved.

Second Line If he finds a temporary base where he can set up his business and hire a loyal assistant, things will turn to his favour.

Third Line Will he lose his temporary base and the loyalty of the people connected with it? Without this harbour he will be in danger.

Fourth Line Even if he gets settled in a provisional home and discovers a way to make his living, he will still have to worry about intruders.

Fifth Line By cultivating the right contacts and doing appropriate favours, he can win the favour of influential people who can help him advance.

Top Line If he loses his home base through carelessness, he may laugh it off at first. But then he realizes that he has nowhere to go and he weeps.

57. Persistent Influence

In this hexagram we are to think of wind with its penetrating power, finding its way into every corner and cranny. ... The superior man, in accordance with this, reiterates his orders and secures the practice of his affairs.

In the long run, only a clear and persistent mind can achieve anything worthwhile. People need a focus in life, a well-defined idea of what ought to be done. As long as they are plagued by confusion and doubts, they will lack staying-power and dissipate their energies. They need the ability to face the facts, to set priorities, to make decisions and to carry them out. They must learn to rise to their daily challenges without fear, like a brave soldier.

But to make the right decisions you need inner clarity and subtlety. As long as you behave violently or desperately, this shows that you are still unsure of yourself and that you are fighting yourself as well as external problems. All hidden doubts must therefore be dealt with first, so that you can act intelligently and with one mind. You can hardly solve such problems by crawling under the bed or by consulting the stars or a crystal ball. Divination has its place, but at this stage it would probably add to the confusion.

Life means change and growth, and like everybody else you will now and then lose your inner clarity. Doubts and confusion have a way of reappearing just when you thought that you had cleared up things once and for all. And if a project starts off on the wrong foot, you still have a chance to straighten it out. Even seemingly hopeless conditions can be turned into interesting challenges and eventual success. What counts is your ability to decide the issues as they come up and to do first things first.

'They must learn to rise to their daily challenges without fear, like a brave soldier.'

Changing Lines

Bottom Line As long as he is full of doubts and unable to decide things, he will accomplish little. He needs to act more like a brave soldier, by setting priorities and doing first things first.

Second Line By evading decisions and crawling into a dark corner he only magnifies his problems. His fate is not primarily in the stars or in a crystal ball, but in his own hands.

Third Line Is his approach violent and desperate? His road will become smoother and his achievements greater as soon as he gains inner clarity and certainty.

Fourth Line When he knows what he wants, beyond doubt, and keeps his goal in mind, he will find success in the inner and outer world.

Fifth Line Even though there may have been confusion at first, he can still turn the project into a success, if he allows time for consultation and gives advance notice to all involved.

Top Line If he loses his ability to make decisions, all is lost. He will sink into fear and darkness, even if he has the best of intentions.

巽下巽上‧巽‧小亨。利有攸往。利見大人。

以巽為德‧是以小亨也。上下皆順巽‧以巽為德‧故申命行也。剛巽乎中正而志行‧柔皆順乎剛‧是以小亨‧利有攸往‧利見大人也。

58. Enjoying Life

When pleasure leads the people on, they forget their toils. The superior man, in accordance with this, encourages the conversation of friends and the stimulus of their common practice.

In this hexagram, joy is symbolized by a smiling lake or by a happy young daughter. People are always searching for happiness, but often they do not know what it is or how it originates. True happiness radiates from within and affects everything a person thinks and does. It is based on inner harmony and inner sincerity, which in turn results in sincere and harmonious relationships and a happy environment.

If people try to increase their enjoyment of life by surrounding themselves with pleasurable objects, they will find no real satisfaction. The sense of novelty wears off after a while, and soon they are left with their inner emptiness. People who depend entirely on others for their happiness are also heading for disappointment. And those who show off their happiness and join other pleasure seekers are merely covering up their inner void and frustration.

In which area should you look for happiness? As long as you are weighing the various alternatives, you are still bothered by doubts and you have not yet found the inner certainty and unity that comes with true contentment. But as soon as you find this inner harmony, your whole life will be pervaded by joy, and everything you think and do will be pleasurable. In this state you have attained the dynamic balance between thoughts and emotions, between head and heart. You are not indiscriminately indulging in euphoria, but you retain a subtle mental balance and sense of proportion. In this way you avoid becoming the victim of childish hopes or deceitful promises, while at the same time enjoying the innocence of the heart and the support of nature.

'... joy is symbolized by a smiling lake or by a happy young daughter.'

Changing Lines

Bottom Line When doubts have been resolved, a feeling of happiness arises by itself, and all he thinks and does is pervaded by inner harmony.

Second Line His confidence and good fortune are the result of inner sincerity. Only by being true to himself and cultivating sincere relationships can he enjoy life.

Third Line If he merely surrounds himself with objects and people in the hope of increasing his pleasure, he will be disappointed and frustrated. True happiness springs from inner harmony.

Fourth Line If, in his search for happiness, he weighs the various alternatives, this shows uncertainty. Real joy comes when he is no longer disturbed by doubts.

Fifth Line Is he going overboard with mindless euphoria? By indiscriminately wallowing in pleasures and pleasant emotions, or by putting his trust in people he does not sufficiently know, he sets the stage for unhappiness.

Top Line By making a show of his happiness and surrounding himself with other vain pleasure-seekers, he demonstrates that he is still an apprentice in the art of enjoying life.

兌上兌下

兌　亨利貞象曰兌說也剛中而柔外說以

59. Disintegration

The figure is made up of one of the trigrams for water and over it that for wind. Wind moving over water seems to disperse it.

Life can be seen as a continuous process of integration and disintegration. In nature, water collects in a lake and is then evaporated through the action of wind and sun, but the rains will soon bring new water. Trees and plants lose their foliage in the fall so that they can grow new leaves in the spring.

Similarly, social and political structures take shape, fulfil their function and then disintegrate. Old arrangements are abandoned to make room for more suitable ones. In the lives of individual people, conditions at home and at work can change unexpectedly. Relationships between people are constantly being formed, revised and dissolved.

Such changes can be a nuisance, a threat, or even a disaster. But a person's attitude can make all the difference. We can, for example, anticipate changes and act accordingly, by withdrawing to a safe area or by obtaining help. Instead of resisting and resenting change, we can welcome it as an essential part of life. Instead of clinging anxiously to our own petty arrangements, we can become aware of the greater scene and other people's problems. We can even transcend traumatic past experiences and fears by abandoning our tense attitude and seeing things in perspective. Instead of fearing disintegration, we can encourage the disintegration of negative emotions, obsolete ideas and outdated arrangements.

巽坎上下渙亨王假有廟利涉大川利貞象曰渙亨

'In nature, water collects in a lake and is then evaporated through the action of wind and sun ...'

Changing Lines

Bottom Line Are the present arrangements beginning to dissolve? When he senses an emergency or danger, he acts fast and uses all the help he can get.

Second Line When the present structure starts to fall apart, he hurries to reach a safe place where he has access to the things that support him.

Third Line Instead of worrying only about his own affairs, he concerns himself with less selfish aims. He becomes aware of other people's problems and dissolves his ego.

Fourth Line When the prevailing arrangements and concepts become obsolete, he lets them dissolve, thus making room for a more suitable order. Few people seem to think of doing this.

Fifth Line When he finds himself amid a crumbling old order, he divides and shares the remaining assets. Then he gathers his energies and creates a new arrangement.

Top Line If his mind is fixed on traumatic past experiences, he abandons his tense attitude and dissolves his anxiety. By putting things into perspective he loses his fear and regains his balance.

巽上坎下渙亨王假有廟利涉大川利貞象曰渙亨

60. Limitations

If the regulations be severe and difficult, they cannot be permanent. The superior man, in accordance with this, constructs his methods of numbering and measurement, and discusses points of virtue and conduct.

A lake contains water and is surrounded by a shore. Bowls are shaped in a certain way so that they can hold food. The days and the seasons follow each other in a set rhythm. Each thing and each person has certain capacities and certain limitations.

As long as we are aware of our limitations, we can make the best of our capabilities. Although the constraints of life are usually experienced as nuisances, they have their function and they are part of life. They keep us fit, slim and alert, and without them we would become soft, dumb and lethargic. By working with them instead of resenting them we can develop thrifty habits and trim needless expenditures. The measured approach is the one that brings happiness, freedom and success in the end.

People who fail to practise a degree of self-mastery or self-discipline soon become slaves of external limitations or authorities. If they demand too much in life, they will always be at the mercy of the forces that limit their desires. If they resent all regulations and demand total freedom, they will fall prey to those who promise to satisfy their childish wishes with the intention of enslaving them.

But this kind of self-control should not lead to a negative and ascetic withdrawal from life. You need to keep in touch with the world and with people. You need to leave your home base now and then, to widen your horizon and to grasp opportunities. To stay in good shape you do not have to starve yourself.

'A lake contains water and is surrounded by a shore. ... Each thing and each person has certain capacities and certain limitations.'

坎兌
上下
節亨苦節不可貞象曰節亨剛柔分而剛

Changing Lines

Bottom Line By spreading his interests and energies too far and too thin he would weaken his control. Therefore he limits his efforts to the area closer to home.

Second Line If his outlook is narrow and negative, he will miss many opportunities. Therefore he leaves his home periodically to explore the world and widen his horizon.

Third Line If he ignores his limits and fails to practise a degree of self-discipline, he will soon find himself in humiliating situations. If he does not follow his own conscience, he will be dominated by external limitations and authorities.

Fourth Line He need not become a slave of rules, conventions and restrictions. By quietly and naturally being aware of inevitable inner and outer limitations, he can remain the master of his fate.

Fifth Line Only by happily accepting certain limitations and by limiting his appetites can he become a free and contented person.

Top Line He can find an approach that is neither too lax nor too severe. If he imposes rigid and difficult roles on himself and/or others, he will provoke discontent and rebellion.

61. The Sincere Heart

Sincerity thus symbolized will transform a country. Sincerity reaches to and affects even pigs and fishes. There will be advantage in crossing the great stream.

This hexagram shows two soft lines in the centre and two hard lines each above and below, symbolizing a sincere heart inside and firm virtue outside. People who are thus guided by sincerity and firm principles have a strong influence on those around them. With their warm-hearted attitude they even touch and motivate persons who are as dumb as pigs and fishes.

When you are thus centred, so that your thoughts and actions originate from your inner source of strength, and your body movements originate from your gravity centre near the hips, you accomplish great things with a minimum of effort. People are naturally attracted to you and eager to share your insights that come from the heart. Because you do not try to manipulate or dominate others, they tend to co-operate with you spontaneously. They sense your unselfish and warm-hearted attitude and they feel comfortable in your company.

But such emotional ties are subject to fluctuations. Pleasant conversation will be followed by silence, and deep understanding by alienation. This is why you need firm principles to keep joy and sorrow from going to extremes. You want to maintain a natural balance between feelings and thoughts, between your heart and your head. Neither the heart nor the head should predominate, they should complement and enhance each other, just like a man and a woman when they really understand each other.

巽上兌下・中孚豚魚吉利涉大川利貞象曰中孚。柔

迎來踍力不如和日到中時便

羅書此外更無消遣事且說地

上一觀魚　卯池漁父畫

'Sincerity reaches to and affects even pigs and fishes.'

Changing Lines

Bottom Line If his thoughts and actions spring from a sincere heart and are carried out with firm conviction, how can anything go wrong? Trouble starts only when he relies too much on external guidance.

Second Line Just as the crane shares its happiness with its young, a sincere and free spirit is willing to share his/her insights with those who are receptive.

Third Line In his closer relationships he is bound to experience joy and sorrow, emotional ups and downs, periods of sharing and periods of silence. But by maintaining firm principles he can avoid excesses.

Fourth Line When emotional ties are growing stronger, he may sometimes be alienated from his companion(s) through no fault of his own. But if the relationship is worthwhile it will soon return to normal.

Fifth Line The attraction of a sincere heart is irresistible. If he is perfectly sincere he will link others to him in closest union. Mutual projects thrive and succeed.

Top Line If his success with others makes him cocky and he keeps trying to rise above them, he will soon be humiliated.

巽上。兌下。中孚豚魚吉利涉大川利貞象曰中孚柔

62. Moderation

震艮
上下
小過亨利貞可小事不可大事飛鳥遺之

It is better for the bird to descend, keeping near to where it can perch and rest, than to hold on ascending into the homeless regions of the air.

Through the symbol of a high-flying bird, this hexagram reminds us of the human tendency to demand too much, to over-react and to mess in other people's affairs. The message is that we are better off if we stay close to home and mind our own business. By sticking our neck out too far or by getting involved in extravagant projects we would only waste our resources, provoke accidents and invite opposition. The people we deal with would soon sense our arrogant attitude and they would resent being dominated or manipulated. And those above us would become aware of our pushy and impertinent ways and put us into our place.

But this does not mean that you should be servile and passive and let others take the initiative. You will find plenty of opportunities to get busy close to home, and many small actions can add up to a great achievement in time.

There will also be occasions when you have to take far-reaching action if your position is affected by changing circumstances. Such actions will be justified and beneficial, as long as you do not over-react or exceed your authority. Your purpose is to get things back to normal, not to set drastic examples or to show your superiority. In the end you achieve more if you use your power with discretion, if you husband your resources and use the moderate approach.

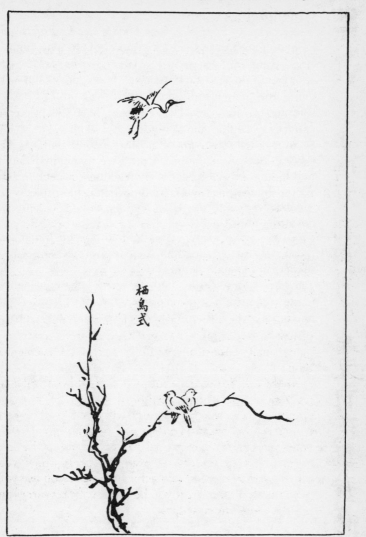

'It is better for the bird to descend, keeping near to where it can perch and rest ...'

觀
上下
小過亨利貞可小事不可大事飛鳥遺之

Changing Lines

Bottom Line By flying too high and demanding too much he invites misfortune. He can find enough opportunities close to home.

Second Line Instead of bothering those above him with unreasonable demands, he thrives by tending his own garden.

Third Line If he is not cautious and attempts too much, those who oppose him will attack his weak spots and injure him.

Fourth Line When the situation requires him to take action, he does not over-react, but he cautiously brings things back to normal. After that he withdraws and does not insist on formalities.

Fifth Line Is he aware of his limitations and his limited resources? By avoiding high and risky projects he will be successful in small matters.

Top Line Domineering and arrogant behaviour would invite opposition and cause accidents. Therefore he minds his own business and does not exceed his proper course.

63. The Fragile Balance

There has been good fortune in the beginning; there may be disorder in the end. The superior man, in accordance with this, thinks of evil that may come and guards against it.

When order has just been established, people tend to become complacent. They are tempted to assume that all problems have now been solved once and for all, or that the new arrangement is so perfect that danger is out of the question. But even a new boat can spring a leak, and the captain must forever be prepared for unexpected cliffs and bad weather.

Whenever a project has been completed and a harmonious balance has been established, the forces of chaos, destruction and decay tend to become active again. Nothing in life stands still, and structures of all kinds are continuously emerging and disappearing. But as long as we are aware of the transitory nature of life, we can act accordingly. We can first of all do much to prevent decay, by watching our weak areas and fortifying weak spots. We can also obtain the necessary materials and tools for fighting decay once it gets underway. Basic know-how and simple devices are often sufficient to do this.

When the disintegrating forces can no longer be stopped, we can minimize our losses by withdrawing to a safer place or to a less vulnerable position. Things may now be so serious that we have to take fast and drastic action to prevent the worst.

When the existing order finally disintegrates, much patience and persistence is needed to create a new foundation and to make a new start. This is best done with the help of strong-minded companions who are fully committed to the goal. Sooner or later a new order will emerge, with all the tendencies described above.

坎上　離下。既濟亨小。利貞、初吉終亂、彖曰既濟亨小

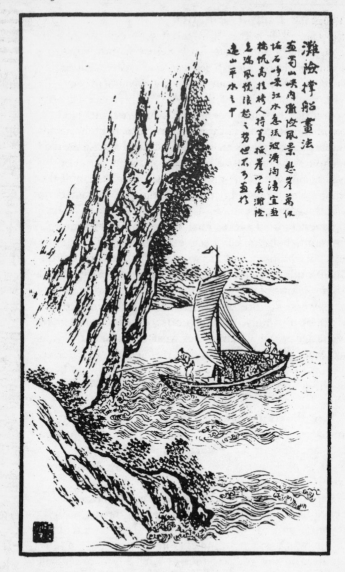

'... even a new boat can spring a leak, and the captain must forever be prepared for unexpected cliffs and bad weather.'

Changing Lines

Bottom Line When the disintegrating forces threaten to take control, he minimizes his losses by withdrawing to a less vulnerable position.

Second Line When curious people invade his privacy, he does not panic. They will soon leave him alone as the sense of loyalty wears off and he keeps his distance.

Third Line Once the established order is lost, he needs patience, persistence and the aid of strong-minded companions to create a new order.

Fourth Line When a boat threatens to develop leaks, materials for repairing them should be obtained in advance. When he senses danger, he provides himself with the means of averting or avoiding it.

Fifth Line A pompous sacrifice is not as effective as a small one offered with sincerity. He can usually accomplish more with simple means and devices than with showy and expensive implements.

Top Line If the chaos spreads, he will soon be in difficulties up to his neck. Therefore he does his utmost to extricate himself before it is too late.

離下
坎上．
既濟。亨小。利貞。初吉終亂．象曰既濟亨小

64. Success Within Reach

The young fox has nearly crossed the stream, but he has not yet escaped from the midst of the danger and calamity. The superior man, in accordance with this, carefully discriminates among things and the positions they occupy.

When the great water has almost been crossed and the opposite shore seems within easy reach, special care is in order to make a safe landing. Similarly, during the final stages of a great project, we need to watch our step to ensure our final success.

There is, for example, the temptation to rush through the final stages of the project like a young and inexperienced fox who impatiently jumps through dangerous waters and almost drowns. An experienced old fox, on the other hand, would keep his eyes and ears open, tread carefully and search for the safest route.

Another pitfall is due to the human tendency to overshoot the goal, to keep forging ahead when the job is almost done. An experienced and well-balanced person knows when to shift to a more subtle mode that introduces the final harmony.

When the project is almost completed we may have to deal firmly with last-minute obstacles or destructive influences that threaten the final success. But at the same time we need to concentrate on the main goal so that we do not get side-tracked by minor issues. And last, but not least, we must avoid the temptation of boasting and celebrating prematurely, when success is not yet certain and much work remains to be done.

'The young fox has nearly crossed the stream but he has not yet escaped ...'

Changing Lines

Bottom Line If he pushes ahead recklessly and forgets his main goal, in the hope of achieving a quick success, humiliation is sure to follow.

Second Line When success is near, he can avoid overshooting his goal by slowing down and carefully adding the final touches. To pursue success he needs one set of virtues, but to maintain it he needs to use the subtle and balanced approach.

Third Line By remembering his greater goal and his desire for a new order, he can avoid getting involved in negative or destructive side issues.

Fourth Line Shortly before the new harmony is established, obstacles or destructive influences may threaten his progress. Resolute action is then called for and will be rewarded by great and lasting success.

Fifth Line During the final stages of his project he needs wisdom and intelligence to bring it to completion. A bright and determined mind can pervade all aspects of the project and bring together the separate efforts.

Top Line If he counts his chickens before they are hatched, he invites disappointment. Through premature boasts and celebrations he will distract his attention from the main goal and reduce his chances of success.

離坎
上下

未濟亨小狐汔濟濡其尾无攸利象曰未

PART THREE

Appendices

Instructions for Quick Reference

Use this page as a quick guide when you throw the coins to find out which answer (hexagram) applies at a given time. For detailed instructions see Chapters 3 and 8.

Build your hexagram from the bottom up by throwing the three coins once for each line. Four combinations are possible:

Two heads and one tail: draw a straight line ——

Two tails and one head: draw a divided line —— ——

Three heads: draw a divided line with an 'X' —— —— x

Three tails: draw a straight line with an 'X' ———— x

Chart for Looking up Your Hexagram

Upper Trigram	Chien	Chen	Kan	Ken	Kun	Sun	Li	Tui
Lower Trigram								
Chien	2	34	5	26	11	9	14	43
Chen	25	51	3	27	24	42	21	17
Kan	6	40	29	4	7	59	64	47
Ken	33	62	39	52	15	53	56	31
Kun	12	16	8	23	1	20	35	45
Sun	44	32	48	18	46	57	50	28
Li	13	55	63	22	36	37	30	49
Tui	10	54	60	41	19	61	38	58

Trace the vertical column down to where it meets the horizontal bar and read the number at the crossing point.

Index of Answers (Hexagrams)

INDEX

Of further interest . . . .

FORTUNE TELLING BY MAH JONGG

Derek Walters — The game of Mah Jongg first arrived in the West at the beginning of the twentieth century, yet its pieces are implements for a system of Chinese divination that goes back more than two thousand years. Derek Walters traces the development of the modern game and explains in detail the symbolism of each of the 144 Mah Jongg tiles. This remarkable system is as complex and subtle as the *I Ching* and can provide answers to an unlimited number of questions on love, business matters, health, career opportunities, and general prospects.

FORTUNE-TELLING
BY DICE
Uncovering the Future Through
the Ancient System of
Casting Lots

FORTUNE TELLING BY DICE

The Three-Colour Method

David and Julia Line – In the *only* book of its kind available
David and Julia Line explain a complete system of fortune-telling,
requiring only three dice of different colours (red, green and
white). Over 650 individual meanings are given for dice thrown in
groups of three in an extensive reference section, and every
possible combination is covered by the 3 categories – 'General
Situation', 'Finance/Business', 'Love/Affection'. With a series of
casebook studies they trace the background to this method of
fortune-telling – and illustrate the accuracy of dice in the
divination scene.

FORTUNE TELLING BY PLAYING CARDS

'Play your cards right' in the game of life.

Nerys Dee – shows how to understand, and profit from, the symbolic messages hidden in a pack of ordinary playing cards.

- Discover hidden personal talents
- Gain emotional and financial security
- Promote personal success

Includes full instructions for 'reading' each card plus a selection of spreads.

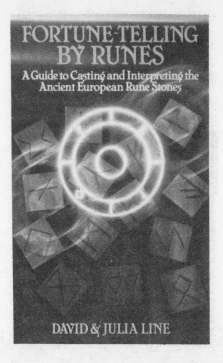

FORTUNE TELLING BY RUNES

David and Jula Line – Casting runes to shed light on the future is one of the least well documented methods of divination, and yet it is one of the easiest, and is remarkable in its accuracy. Here is an essentially practical book, containing all the information needed to cast rune stones and to interpret individual and group meanings from where the stones fall on a runic chart. The authors demonstrate the simplicity of the techniques involved and show that anyone can learn to use the runes to discover the secret of what their future holds.

FORTUNE TELLING BY TAROT CARDS

An Easy to Read Introduction

Sasha Fenton – a professional Tarot reader – has called upon her years of experience to produce this down-to-earth, no-nonsense guide to understanding and interpreting the Tarot. Aimed at the complete beginner, her explanations are at all times clear and easy to understand. Includes three levels of spread, simple, complicated and special purposes, provides details of a 'timing device' to determine when events will take place, plus a 'quick-clue' section which gives key – word meanings for each card. This is a book to be read, then kept by the cards as a handy reference guide. *Illustrated with 'Prediction' cards but suitable for any standard deck.*